Adventures in Art

Laura H. Chapman

Davis Publications, Inc.

Worcester, Massachusetts

Front cover: *Student artwork by Santos Avila, Mensendick School, Glendale, Arizona. From the Crayola® Dream-Makers® Collection, courtesy of Binney & Smith Inc.*

Title page: *Fletcher Martin, Glory. Oil on canvas, 34 x 48" (86 x 122 cm). Edwin A. Ulrich Museum of Art, The Wichita State University (Gift of Mr. and Mrs. Robert Blauner).*

Editorial Advisory Board:

Dr. Cynthia Colbert
Professor of Art
and Chair of Art Education
University of South Carolina
Columbia, South Carolina

Bill MacDonald
Art Education Consultant
Vancouver, British Columbia
Canada

Dr. Connie Newton
Assistant Professor of Art
School of Visual Art
University of North Texas
Denton, Texas

Sandra Noble
Curriculum Specialist for the Fine Arts
Cleveland Public Schools
Cleveland, Ohio

Reading Consultant:

Dr. JoAnn Canales
College of Art Education
University of North Texas
Denton, Texas

Reviewers:

Cliff Cousins
Art Specialist
Davenport Community School District
Davenport, Iowa

Dr. Lila G. Crespin
College of Fine Art
California State University at
Long Beach

Lee Gage
Art Supervisor
Westchester Area School District
Westchester, Pennsylvania

William Gay, Jr.
Visual Art Coordinator
Richland County School District One
Columbia, South Carolina

Dr. Adrienne W. Hoard
Associate Professor
University of Missouri-Columbia

Mary Jordan
Visual Arts Curriculum Specialist
Tempe, Arizona

Kathleen Lockhart
Curriculum & Instructional Specialist
Baltimore, Maryland

David McIntyre
Consultant for Visual Arts
El Paso Independent School District
El Paso, Texas

R. Barry Shauck
Supervisor of Art
Howard County Public School
Ellicott City, Maryland

Linda Sleight
Visual Arts Curriculum Specialist
Tempe, Arizona

Carl Yochum
Director of Fine Arts
Ferguson-Florissant School District
Florissant, Missouri

Joyce Young
Assistant Principal
Bond Hill School
Cincinnati, Ohio

Acknowledgements:
The author and publisher would like to thank the following individuals and groups for their special assistance in providing images, resources and other help: Tom Feelings, Mickey Ford, Claire Mowbray Golding, Colleen Kelley, Samella Lewis, Maya Nigrosh, Sandra Palmer, Dawn Reddy, Tara Reddy, Patricia A. Renick, Chloë Sayer, Martha Siegel, Martin Speed, Bernice Steinbaum, Anne Straus, and art teachers in the Department of Defense Dependent Schools.

Managing Editor:
Wyatt Wade

Editor:
Laura J. Marshall

Design:
Douglass Scott, WGBH Design

Production:
Nancy Dutting

Photo Acquisitions:
Allan Harper

Illustrator:
Susan Christy-Pallo

Photography:
Schlowsky Photography

Contents

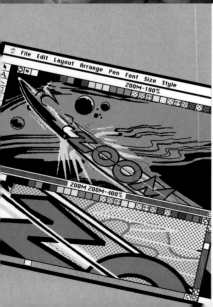

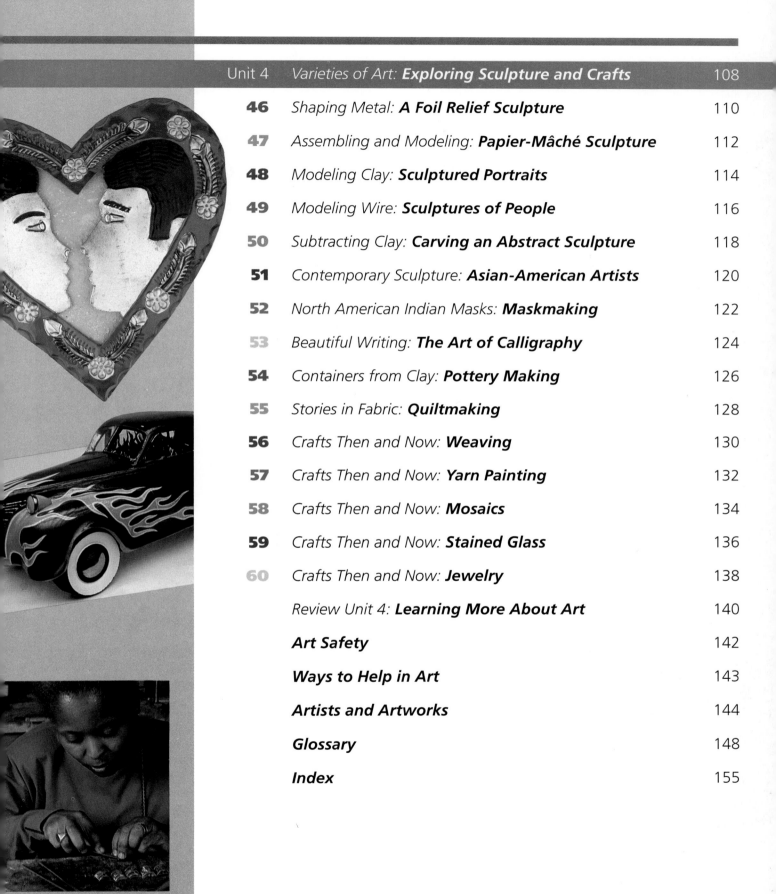

Seeing and Creating Art
Design in Art

 A   Photograph: R. Chen, Superstock, Inc.

B   **William van Alen,** *Chrysler Building,* New York, 1928–30.
Photograph: Carolyn Schaefer, Superstock, Inc.

Your world is full of wonders. During most of the day, you see things in a way that allows you to do a chore or to go from place to place. When you see your world as an **artist**, your eyes focus on the beauty and wonder in your world.

Art is a combination of many skills and ideas. One of the most important skills is thinking about what you see. Thinking and seeing as an artist means you use your **imagination**. You make pictures in your mind of things you see, feel and know. When you create art you can share your visions with others.

You can see wonderful things in the **natural environment**. The photograph in picture A is one small example. Why do you think the photographer found this scene so fascinating?

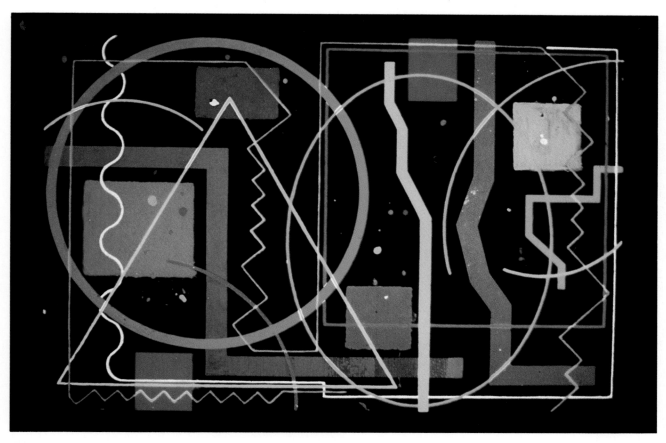

Tom Bacher, *Moderné, No. 11,* 1990. Phosphorescent acrylic on canvas, 36 x 54" (81 x 139 cm). Cincinnati Art Galleries.

You can see strange and beautiful things in the constructed world too. The **constructed environment** is everything people have added to nature. Look at the photograph in picture B. Why do you think the artist wanted to record this view of the buildings?

In this book, you will learn how artists see and think as they create art. You will learn why artists plan their work and how they do experiments.

When artists plan their work, they must see and think about the elements and principles of design. The **elements of design** are: line, shape, color, texture, space, form and value (light and dark).

Artists also use ideas known as principles of design to plan their work. A principle of design is a guide for relating the visual elements. Some **principles of design** are: balance, rhythm, proportion, pattern, emphasis, unity and variety.

 Sierras, California. Superstock, Inc.

B **Charles Sheeler, *Skyscrapers,*** 1922. Oil on canvas, 20 x 13"
(51 x 33 cm). ©The Phillips Collection, Washington, DC.

You can learn to look for pictures to draw or paint. You can plan the shapes of the pictures you create. Use a viewfinder to find ideas for your artwork. A **viewfinder** is a sheet of paper with a hole in it.

Artists plan their drawings and paintings. They can plan a tall, vertical picture. They can plan a wide, horizontal picture. Some artists like to make pictures inside of squares and other shapes.

Charles Sheeler, a United States artist, created the paintings in pictures B and C. Picture B is composed inside a **vertical** rectangle. The tall, narrow shape helps to emphasize the feeling of tall buildings crowded together in a city.

Charles Sheeler, *Architectural Cadences,* 1954. 25 x 35" (64 x 89 cm). Collection of Whitney Museum of American Art, New York.

Now look at the painting in picture C. Why do you think the artist chose a **horizontal** rectangle for his painting? What does the shape of the painting help him emphasize? Why do you think this artist liked to show buildings and cityscapes in his artwork?

You can learn to plan the shapes of your pictures. Make sketches of something in the classroom or outside the window. Make each sketch a different shape.

Make a viewfinder from an index card. Fold the card in half. Cut a hole in the center of the fold about 1/2" (1 cm) deep and 3/4"(2 cm) wide. Save your viewfinder for other lessons.

D

Keeping a Sketchbook
Why Artists Sketch

 Leonardo da Vinci, *Star of Bethlehem, with Crowsfoot and Wood Anemone,* ca. 1505–07. Red chalk, pen and ink, 7 3/4 x 6 1/4" (20 x 16 cm). Windsor Castle, Royal Library. ©1992 Her Majesty Queen Elizabeth II.

 Leonardo da Vinci, *Studies for an Equestrian Monument,* ca. 1517–18. Windsor Castle, Royal Library. ©1992 Her Majesty Queen Elizabeth II.

Many artists make sketches as a way to explore ideas for art. A **sketch** is often a drawing an artist makes to plan an artwork. Artists also make sketches to record and remember things they see.

Many sketches are created quickly and never become a finished artwork. The sketches are made to record an idea, just as you make written notes to remember ideas.

Some artists combine sketches with written notes.

One of the most well-known sketchbooks was created about 500 years ago by Leonardo da Vinci, an Italian artist. He sketched rivers, clouds, animals and flowers. His sketches show his inventions, such as a helicopter and submarine. Drawings from two pages in his sketchbooks are shown in pictures A and B. Why do you think he made the sketches?

Henry Spencer Moore, *Madonna and Child,* 1943. Pen and ink and wash drawing, 8 7/8 x 6 7/8" (23 x 18 cm). The Cleveland Museum of Art (Hinman B. Hurlbut Collection).

Henry Spencer Moore, *Madonna and Child,* 1943–44. Hornton stone, 59" (150 cm) high. Church of St. Mathew, Northhampton, England. Photograph: National Buildings Record, London.

Compare pictures C and D. These artworks were created by the English artist, Sir Henry Moore. Notice how the two sketches capture the feeling of **three-dimensional** forms. Which sketch is most like the sculpture? What differences are there in the sculpture and the sketches?

You will be asked to make sketches for many art lessons. You can draw them in a sketchbook or a notebook. You will make sketches to explore ideas and plan artworks. Some of your sketches will show things you observe and think about.

Sketching can be fun. You can practice sketching at home and other places such as shopping malls, parks and playgrounds. The more you practice sketching, the more you discover about your visual world.

A Crayon Etching
Exploring Lines and Textures

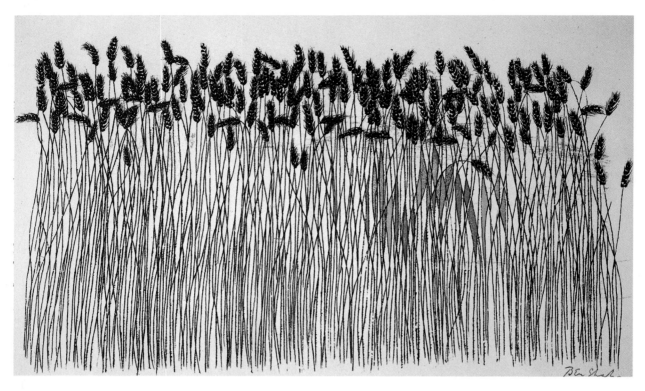

A   **Ben Shahn, *Wheat Field,*** 1958. Hand-colored screenprint. National Gallery of Art, Washington, DC (Rosenwald Collection).

There are many ways to get ideas for artwork. Try drawing things you see in nature. This is an important way to get ideas. As you draw, try different ways to show the character of natural forms.

Ben Shahn's artwork in picture A captures the thin, delicate lines of wheat stalks. Thick lines show the shape and texture of wheat tassels. How does he suggest that the tassels are heavy?

Charles Burchfield's crayon drawing in picture B shows a thistle plant. Thistle is a prickly weed with flowers. What **lines** help you see these qualities?

Find a leaf, twig, shell or similar natural form. Draw the main shapes very lightly, then sketch the **edges** in more detail. Use your pencil in different ways. Create lines that show whether your object is delicate or strong, rough or smooth, heavy or light.

Create another version of your drawing using a different **medium**, such as crayon or felt-tipped markers. You might try the technique that students used to create the artwork in picture D. A **technique** is a planned way to do something.

The student artworks in picture D are crayon etchings. **Etching** means you scratch

Charles Burchfield, *Study of Thistle,* 1961. Crayon, 13 1/4 x 18 7/8" (34 x 48 cm).
Collection of Whitney Museum of American Art, New York.

 Student artwork.

into a surface. Crayon etchings are done in the following way.

1. Use a light color of wax crayon or oil pastel. Cover the whole paper with a thick layer.

2. Color the whole paper again with black or another dark color.

3. Use a nail to scratch through the dark color so the light color shows.

You might try different line qualities before you begin your work (see picture C).

When you have finished, compare your pencil drawing and your second artwork. If you like one artwork more than the other, try to explain why.

4

Op Art
Lines Create Illusions

Do you remember when you first learned to draw straight and curved lines to make the letters of the alphabet? Do you recall when you first learned to write words by "drawing" curved lines with loops? Today, handwriting may be so easy that you don't think about the lines and shapes in each letter.

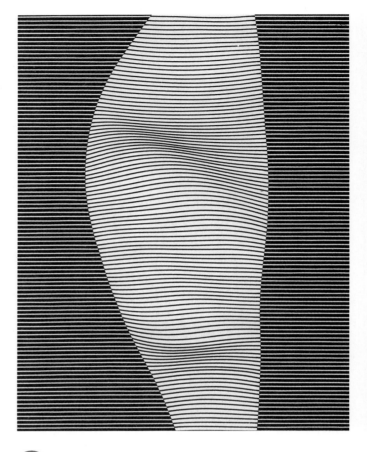

McDonald Bane, *D-1-67 (Santa Ana, California)*, 1967. Pen and brush and ink, 18 3/4 x 24 1/8" (48 x 61 cm). Collection, The Museum of Modern Art, New York (Given anonymously).

When you create artwork, you need to develop new habits of drawing lines and shapes. You need to think about the direction of the lines. You need to see the shapes created by lines and the **spacing** between lines and shapes.

The artworks in this lesson show how artists control the direction and spacing of lines to create optical illusions. This style of artwork is called Op art. (**Op** is a short word for optical.)

Study the example of Op art in picture A. Look at the **parallel** lines near the left and right edges. As your eyes move toward the center, you see gradual changes in the straight lines. The changes are curves or angles. The changes create an **illusion** of forms and motions on a flat surface.

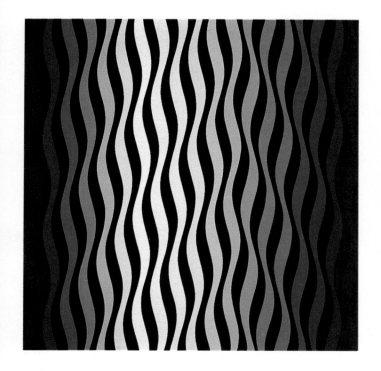

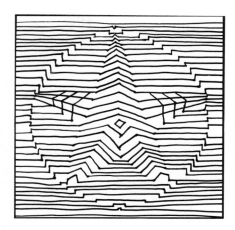

B

Bridget Riley, *Drift No. 2,* 1966. Acrylic on canvas, 91 1/2 x 89 1/2" (232 x 227 cm). Albright-Knox Art Gallery, Buffalo, New York (Gift of Seymour H. Knox).

C

Student artwork.

When you look at the artwork in picture B, you probably see the light and dark wavy lines first. Can you also find wave-like **diagonal** edges that move upward like an upside-down V? What kind of illusion do these lines create?

Students created the artworks in picture C. The artwork at the top was made by using a pencil to lightly sketch a star inside a circle. Then the **horizontal** and angular lines were sketched. To finish the

artwork, marker lines were drawn over the pencil lines.

The second artwork is a **collage**. The design was cut and pasted on colored paper. The wide lettering spells out PS1 inside a triangle. The horizontal lines go across and around the edges of the lettering. How was the collage completed? Can you think of other ways to explore ideas related to Op art?

5

Positive and Negative Shapes
Shapes Create Illusions

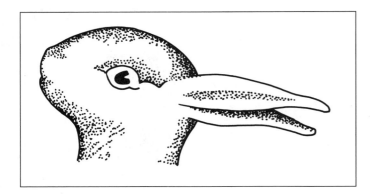

A

B

C

Logo for National Aquarium. Courtesy of Chermayeff and Geismar, Inc.

Your eyes and mind work together. Your mind can help you see things in more than one way. Look at picture A. Name the first thing you see. Did your mind help you see a duck or a rabbit? Look at picture B. What do you see first? Can you find another way to see the image?

Pictures A and B are well-known visual **illusions**. There are many more. You can learn about them by studying science books

that explain how people see and think. You can also learn more about visual illusions by studying artworks.

Artists often create designs that have illusions. For example, in picture C, an artist has created a logo for the National Aquarium. A **logo** is like a trademark. The design has wide shapes that you can see as fish, or waves, or both. Why might the designer want people to see the dark and light shapes in two ways?

There are many variations of this kind of visual illusion. In picture D, the artist

5.

8. The largest of the Rocs picks her up by the skirt.

E **Gustave Verbeek,** illustration from ***The Incredible Upside-Downs of Gustave Verbeek.*** ©1963 The Rajah Press.

D ***Pictopatterns: Snowy Heron,*** from *Visual Elements 1/Pictograms.* ©1988 by Rockport Publishers, Inc., Rockport, Massachusetts.

has created puzzle-like shapes of birds. The edges of the birds fill the white and dark shapes. Do you see how the birds are alike and different?

The artwork in picture E can also be seen in more than one way. The drawing is from a book that illustrates two stories. The main characters are different too. How must you look at the drawing to see the second illustration?

The visual illusions in this lesson show how images can be planned so that you see some shapes or spaces first. When you look again, you see other shapes or spaces. Artists call the areas you see first **positive shapes or spaces**. The areas you see later are called **negative shapes or spaces**.

Create a drawing or a collage with positive and negative areas. Make some sketches first. You might work with another student to get ideas. Sometimes you can get ideas by cutting or drawing looping or zigzag shapes, like a puzzle. Can you explain why this might be a good way to begin?

 Thomas Hart Benton, *Cradling Wheat,* 1938. Tempera and oil on board, 30 11/16 x 37 5/8" (79 x 97 cm). The St. Louis Art Museum (Purchase).

Do you like to hear rhythms in music? Do you like to dance? There are different kinds of rhythm in music, dance and art. In art, a **visual rhythm** comes from repeated lines, shapes or other elements.

The painting in picture A was created by Thomas Hart Benton, a well-known artist from Missouri. The painting shows people harvesting wheat. Do you see the visual rhythms?

Many of the rhythms are created by curves. Can you find some repeated curves? What ideas or feelings do the curved rhythms help to express? Why?

You can also see visual rhythms in picture D. This artwork is a woodcut print. It was created by Hokusai, a well-known artist from Japan. In this artwork, long wavy lines lead your eye downward along the path of the waterfall. What other repeated curves create a feeling of rhythm?

Why do you think artists from very different cultures planned their work to have visual rhythms with strong curves?

In this lesson, you have learned to see and analyze rhythm as a **principle of design**. Now think of a theme or subject that you can express by using this principle of design.

C

D

Hokusai, *The Yoshitsune Horse-Washing Waterfall,* ca. 1831–32. Woodcut, 14 5/8 x 10 3/32" (38 x 26 cm). Collection of the Montreal Museum of Fine Arts (Purchase, John W. Tempest Fund). Photograph: Marilyn Aitken, MMFA.

Designs Express Motions
Nonobjective Art

A **Oscar Howe, *Indian in Nature,*** 1970. Casein on paper. From the Collection of the Heard Museum, Phoenix , Arizona. ©Adelheid Howe, 1992.

The artworks in this lesson are done in a Nonobjective style. In a **Nonobjective** artwork, there are no recognizable objects or scenes. The artist wants you to react to the lines, shapes and other design elements. The artworks in this lesson are designed to imply, or suggest, **movement**.

Look at the artwork in picture A. The artist, Oscar Howe, is a North American Indian of Sioux heritage. His painting is

dominated by curved lines and shapes that imply swirling motion. The movement in his painting comes from his feelings about the beauty of curves in nature. He likes to observe the motions of birds in flight, leaping flames and wind-swept clouds.

Mel Bochner's drawing in picture B is filled with straight, **diagonal** lines. The lines create small and large angular shapes. Many of the lines go toward or away from

each other, as if they are tugging against each other. The title, *Vertigo,* means dizzy, or the feeling that you may fall. What other titles might go with this artwork? Why?

Burgoyne Diller created the painting in picture C. He knew that **vertical** and **horizontal** lines usually make a design look still, or static. His design creates a different kind of implied movement. Look for lines, shapes and colors that seem to **advance**, or move toward you. What parts seem to

recede, or move away from you? Can you explain how the artist implied this to-and-fro motion?

Think of a motion or feeling you could communicate in a Nonobjective artwork. Sketch some designs to discover how lines and shapes can imply, or suggest, motions and feelings. Then choose your best design and create a more finished work. Can your choice of colors also imply movement? How? Why?

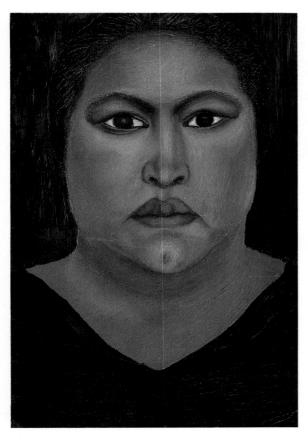

A

Angel Torres Jaramillo (TEBO), *Portrait of My Mother,* 1937. Oil on cardboard, 9 1/8 x 6 1/8" (23 x 16 cm). Collection, The Museum of Modern Art, New York (The Latin American Collection, Gift of Samuel A. Lewisohn, by exchange).

B

Today you will practice drawing faces. Artists learn to draw faces by looking at people carefully. Artists see differences in people's noses, eyes, lips and other features.

When you draw a face, observe the overall shape of the head and neck. For example, in picture A the artist observed the thick neck with a wide jaw and cheeks. The bottom half of the face is like a triangle with rounded edges. The top part of the head is like a half-circle. A different person might have a narrow face and a thin neck. What are some other differences you might see in faces?

Faces are also alike in many ways. The straight lines in picture B are **guidelines** for drawing proportions in the face. A **proportion** shows how one part is related to other parts, or to the whole.

How do the guidelines in picture B help you to draw:

1. the shape of the whole face?
2. the eyes?
3. the top and bottom of nose and ears?
4. the lips?
5. the forehead and hairline?

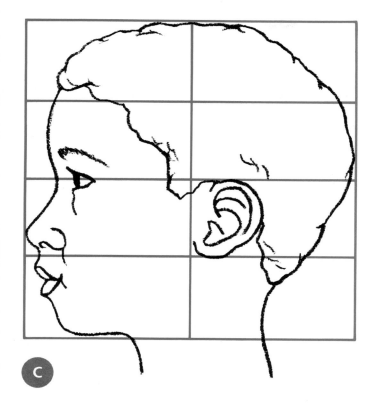

C

D

Albrecht Dürer, *Four Heads,* 1513. Pen and ink, 8 1/4 x 7 7/8" (21 x 20 cm). The Nelson-Atkins Museum of Art, Kansas City, Missouri (Nelson Fund).

A side view of a face is called a **profile**. Sometimes artists draw guidelines before they draw a profile of a face. These guidelines can help you to draw:

1. the shape of the whole face
2. the eyes
3. the top and bottom of nose and ears
4. the lips
5. the forehead and hairline

Draw a front view or profile of a face. You can fold paper to set up guidelines quickly (see picture E). If you draw a profile, begin with a square sheet of paper.

Draw all the main parts of the face first. Draw lightly with a pencil. Then change the lines so your drawing is a portrait. A portrait is an artwork that looks like a real person.

The profile drawings in picture D were created about 500 years ago by a German artist. The profiles behind the first one are caricatures. A **caricature** is an artwork that exaggerates how something actually looks. Why is the first profile more like a portrait than a caricature?

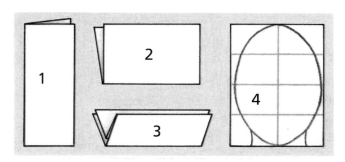

E

9 Unusual Proportions
Using Your Imagination

Have you ever seen elephants with birds' legs? Have you ever seen birds' legs as tall and skinny as those in picture A?

The artworks in this lesson show how unexpected proportions can create a feeling of **fantasy**. Sometimes unusual proportions can be used for humor. They can also be used to express other feelings, such as loneliness or fear.

The Spanish artist, Salvador Dali, created the artwork in picture A. His drawing is a design for an opera backdrop.

Salvador Dali was a leader of an art style called surrealism. **Surrealism** means that an artwork combines realism and dream-like ideas. Many parts of the work are things you can recognize, but they are not combined in an expected way.

Look again at the scenery in picture A. How does the artist suggest a fantasy landscape around the animals? Can you find other examples of unexpected proportions? What else do you see? What feelings do you have as you look at this artwork?

A Salvador Dali, *The Elephants Design for the Opera La Dama Spagnola e il Cavaliere Romano,* 1961. Pencil, watercolor and gouache, 27 1/2 x 27 1/2" (70 x 70 cm). ©1992 Indianapolis Museum of Art (Gift of Mr. and Mrs. Lorenzo Alvary).

Most people have strange dreams at some time. The painting in picture B shows a boy with a man's arms and face. He seems to be sitting comfortably on rocks near a quiet sea.

Some people wonder why the face looks so calm. Other people wonder why the rocks look like a mountain range. How do you interpret this artwork? What else makes the scene look strange?

The French artist who created this painting, Henri Rousseau, taught himself to create paintings. He was a **self-taught artist**. In this painting, he wanted to capture a feeling he had as a boy. What feeling do you think he wanted to express?

Think of a special feeling or idea that you can express by using unexpected proportions. Your idea might come from something very funny or very strange that you remember. You can make up an imaginary time, place or character.

B **Henri Rousseau, *Boy on the Rocks,*** 1895–97. Oil on canvas, 21 3/4 x 18" (55 x 46 cm). National Gallery of Art, Washington, DC (Chester Dale Collection).

Printing Patterns
Patterns from Many Lands

Africa-Egypt

Greece

Italy-Pompeii

Oceania

Do you like to see lines and shapes that create patterns? Many people do. In almost every time and land, people have decorated things with **patterns**.

Patterns can be **allover designs**, such as those you see repeated on fabrics, carpets and wallpaper. Patterns can also be **border** designs around the edges of floors, walls or scarves.

Sometimes patterns include visual symbols. The flower in the pattern from Egypt is a **symbol** for the papyrus plant that grows by the Nile River. In ancient times it was a symbol for royalty. In many lands, organic lines and shapes are used for patterns. **Organic** means that you see curves similar to natural forms such as flowers, vines and leaves. Why do you think organic shapes often appear in patterns?

Most of these patterns look like they were planned with a ruler, a compass or a grid. Artists say the designs have a **geometric** quality. Can you find some geometric shapes such as circles, half-circles, squares and diamonds? Where do you see organic lines and shapes?

These patterns, and many more, were gathered in the 1850s by Albert Racinet, a French artist and historian. He believed artists should know about designs from many cultures, past and present. Do you agree? Why or why not?

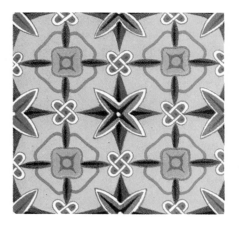

Persia (Middle East)

India

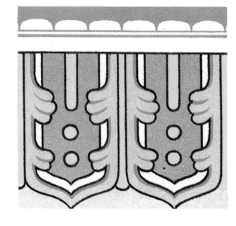

China

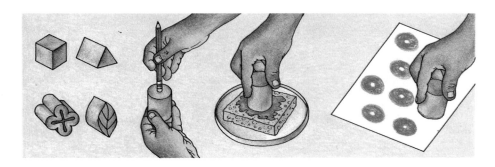

B

Look for other patterns. You can make and print clay stamps to create an allover pattern. An allover pattern covers a whole surface such as paper or cloth. Fold your paper to make a grid. Use the creases as a guide for repeating the design.

C Student artwork.

11 Shapes and Spaces
Printing a Stencil Picture

 Unknown, *Bear in a Tree,* ca. 1850. Stencil. National Gallery of Art, Washington, DC (Gift of Edgar William and Bernice Chrysler Garbisch). Photograph: Dean Beasom.

Have you ever made or used a stencil? A **stencil** is a sheet of paper or other thin material with a shape cut into it. This shape is **printed** by applying ink or paint through the hole.

Over 2,000 years ago, artists in China used stencils to decorate books and walls of temples.

During the Middle Ages in Europe, stencils were used to print playing cards and sheet music. In the South Pacific, artists of the Fiji Islands print designs on cloth. They cut their stencils from dried banana leaves.

In North America, colonists used stencils to print decorations on walls and furniture. Picture A shows a painting with stenciled elements. It was probably created by a family member for a wall at home. Sometimes stencils were combined to create several related pictures with different designs.

Stencils similar to those in picture B were a starting point for *Bear in a Tree.* The open area of a stencil is usually stippled with paint.

When you **stipple** a surface, you tap a stiff brush or sponge up and down to create many tiny dots of color. You can also use chalk or crayons to fill in the shape.

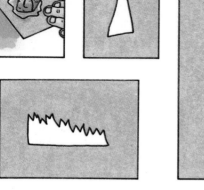

B

The artwork in picture A has many stenciled shapes. Some parts were added without using a stencil. For example, the small branches and clumps of leaves were added without using a stencil. Can you guess how? Where else do you see stenciled and unstenciled areas?

Now look at picture C, created by three students who worked together. What theme did they select? Where did they use stencils? What other ideas did they use?

How is this artwork similar to picture A? How is it different? What is a fair way to judge both artworks?

C Student artwork.

Peter Hurd, *The Gate and Beyond,* 1952. Egg tempera on panel, 47 x 90" (119 x 229 cm). Permanent Collection, Roswell Museum and Art Center (Gift of the artist).

Your world is a three-dimensional **space**. You can see up, down and around. You can also see things that are near or distant.

In many realistic artworks, artists want to create the illusion of depth or distance in space. They learn techniques of perspective to create this kind of illusion. **Perspective** techniques help you draw or paint pictures that show three-dimensional spaces.

There are many perspective techniques. One of them is shown in picture A. The painting shows a landscape with a horizon line. The **horizon line** is the line where the sky meets the ground. Can you find this line in the painting? What objects block your view of part of the horizon line? Why?

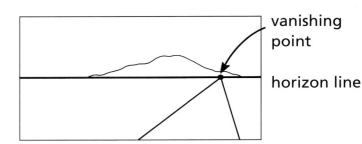

vanishing point

horizon line

Now look at the road in the painting. Can you find the vanishing point? The **vanishing point** is the place where the edges of the road come together or "vanish" from sight. Can you explain why the road looks narrower as it goes toward the horizon line?

vanishing
point

horizon
line

C

Overlap the shapes. Draw the nearest shapes first so that they overlap the distant shapes.

Arrange the shapes. Draw the nearest shapes close to the bottom of the page.

Change the size of the shapes. Draw the nearest shapes larger than the distant shapes.

Study the photograph in picture C. How can you tell that one person is closer than the other? How can you tell that the hills are behind both people? Why can the vanishing point be outside of the edge of a picture?

There are other techniques of perspective drawing. Some of them are shown in picture D.

Practice doing perspective drawings at home and in your neighborhood. Cut out some photographs from magazines. See if you can analyze how they show perspective.

 D

Pierre Bonnard, *The Palm,* 1926. Oil on canvas, 45 x 57 7/8" (114 x 147cm).
©The Phillips Collection, Washington, DC.

Pierre Bonnard, a French artist, created this painting. He mixed colors of paint to show a bright, sunny day. You can mix many colors from the **primary** colors: red, yellow and blue.

When you mix two primary colors together, you get secondary colors. **Secondary** colors are orange, violet and green. Orange is a mixture of yellow and red. What two primary colors can you mix to make violet? and green? Can you find these secondary colors in the painting? Where do you see secondary colors on the color wheel?

Pierre Bonnard has also used many intermediate colors in his painting. **Intermediate** colors are colors such as blue-green and yellow-green.

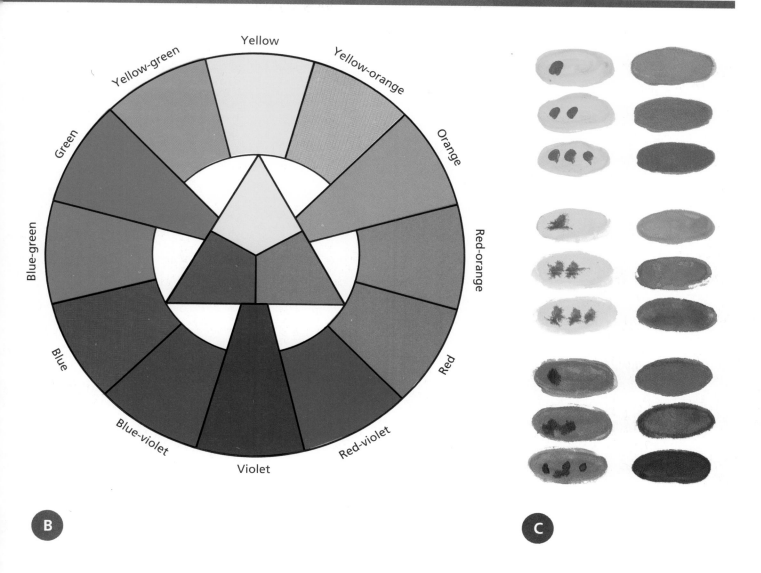

Yellow

Yellow-green · Yellow-orange

Green · Orange

Blue-green · Red-orange

Blue · Red

Blue-violet · Red-violet

Violet

B

C

Almost all of the **hues** in the color wheel can be seen in Bonnard's painting. Many of the light hues in the painting are tints. **Tints** are created by mixing white paint with a color. Where do you see dark colors, or **shades**? Why are the shades located in some spaces and not others?

If you look closely, you can see some of the **brushstrokes**. How do the brushstrokes help to create the illusion of shimmering light and color?

Use the "dot" system to practice mixing secondary and intermediate hues. After you have done some experiments, create a colorful painting of an outdoor scene. Try to combine elements of nature, such as trees or grass, with buildings, highways or other features that people have added to the environment.

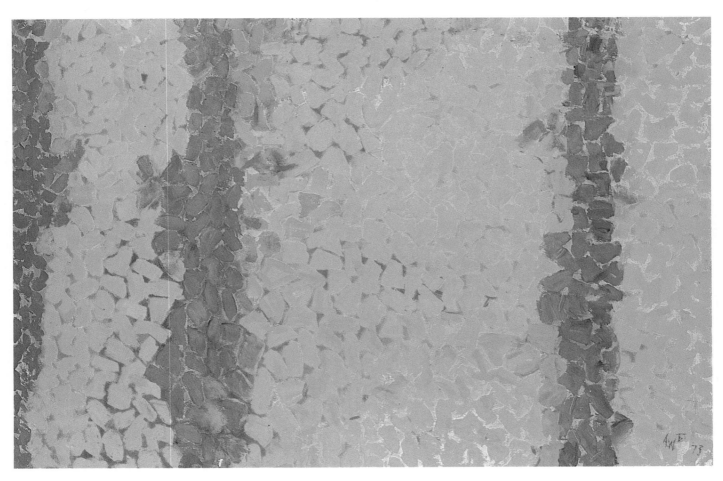

Alma Thomas, *Wind and Crepe Myrtle Concerto,* 1973. Synthetic polymer on canvas, 35 x 52" (89 x 132 cm). National Museum of American Art, Smithsonian Institution, Washington, DC (Gift of Vincent Melzac).

Have you ever seen leaves and flowers "dancing" in the wind? Have you ever imagined the kind of music that might go with colors and motions? Many artists know how to see and imagine things like this.

Alma Thomas, an African-American artist, created the painting in picture A. Many of her paintings can be compared to the rhythms of music or movements of dancers. She often created paintings that seem to "dance" with colors and patterns. Some of her paintings were inspired by the springtime burst of color in the gardens and parks of her hometown, Washington, DC.

Most of the colors in this painting are tints. A **tint** is made by mixing white with another color. This painting has many analogous, or related, tints. **Analogous** colors are next to each other on the color wheel (see page 33).

Stanton Macdonald-Wright, a United States artist, studied in Paris, France in the early 1900s. With other artists, he wanted to combine ideas from music and art. His paintings have abstract shapes with related colors. He thought that colors and shapes could have a visual "harmony" similar to harmony in music.

The title of his painting shown here refers to "colors that go together" much as sounds go together in a symphony. Many of the shapes have been painted in analogous colors. The dark colors are shades. A **shade** is made by mixing a color with black.

B

Stanton Macdonald-Wright, *"Conception" Synchromy,* 1915. Oil on canvas, 30 x 24" (76 x 61 cm). Collection of Whitney Museum of American Art, New York (Gift of George F. Of). Photograph: Geoffrey Clements, New York.

Choose several analogous colors and create a painting. Use tints and shades to create a "harmonious" composition. In art, **harmony** means that visual elements are related to each other like sounds in music or movements in a dance.

When you mix tints, begin with white paint. Add just a little color and mix it. When you mix shades, begin with the color, then add a little black. Can you explain why these steps can help you mix paints?

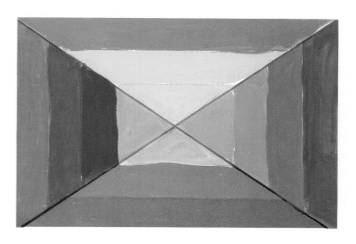

C   Student artwork.

Styles of Painting
A View Out the Window

French artist Pierre Bonnard is one of many painters who worked in the style of **Impressionism**. Paintings in this style have light and color as the main idea. Impressionists wanted to show the subtle colors of a clear morning or an overcast day. They often painted quickly so they could capture colors and patterns of light before they changed.

Pierre Bonnard's painting is filled with warm and cool colors. **Warm** colors are varieties of red, yellow and orange. **Cool** colors are varieties of blue, green and violet. Everything in this room and outside is "bathed" in light colors that are warm or cool. The whole composition seems to capture a quiet, sleepy mood.

Pretend you are the artist and planning this painting. Would you sketch every detail before you started painting? Why or why not? What colors would you mix and use first? Why? Where would you put these colors? What brushstrokes would you use?

A **Pierre Bonnard,** *Open Window,* 1921. Oil on canvas, 46 1/2 x 37 3/4" (118 x 96 cm). ©The Phillips Collection, Washington, DC.

Henri Matisse and Pierre Bonnard knew each other. They were almost the same age. They often created artwork about similar subjects but each artist worked in a different style. Matisse is known as a leader of a style called **Expressionism**. He uses strong, or intense, colors. His bold lines, shapes and patterns express energy and excitement.

Matisse's painting has many very dark and very light colors. The curtain at the right has a bold African design. A solid black shadow is used to outline the window and bring out the form of the bowl. One critic said the palm tree is made of "explosive" brushstrokes with "branches whizzing like rockets."

With several classmates, discuss and identify other similarities and differences in these paintings. After you have discussed these artworks, create a painting of a view out of a window. Use brushstrokes, colors and other design elements in your own special **style**. How will you plan your painting?

B **Henri Matisse, *Interior with Egyptian Curtain,*** 1948. Oil on canvas, 45 3/4 x 35 1/8" (116 x 89 cm). ©The Phillips Collection, Washington, DC.

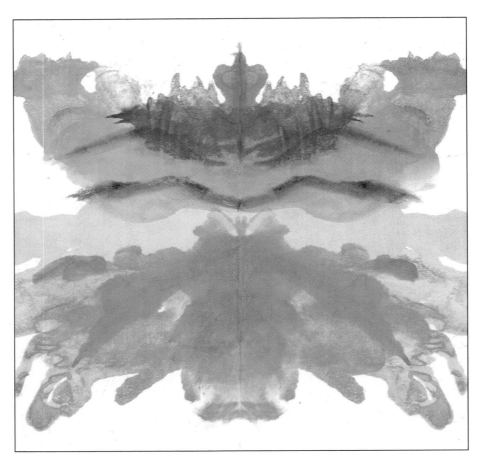

Ⓐ **Joan M. Cochrane, *Freedom,*** 1991. Watercolor. Courtesy of the artist.

This lesson gives you an outline for discussing your own and others' art. Experts use ideas in this outline to see and understand artworks.

The statements in italic are examples of ideas that go with picture A. Many of the art words are defined in the glossary and other lessons. You can find the lessons by using the index.

Step 1. Describe what you see. Take time to look at the artwork. The credit line may help you answer questions a, b, c and d.

a. What kind of art is this? (*a painting*)

b. Who created the artwork? When? (*Joan M. Cochrane, 1991*)

c. How large is the original artwork? (*unknown*)

d. What materials did the artist use? (*watercolor*)

e. How did the artist use the materials? (*The paint looks very watery.*)

f. What are the main design elements?

- Lines (*straight center line, uneven outlines*)
- Shapes (*blending together, irregular edges*)
- Colors (*cool near top, warm near bottom*)
- Textures (*soft, fuzzy*)
- Spaces (*same on both sides of center*)
- Values (*white background, dark colors at the top*)

g. What subjects can you recognize? (*You can't tell exactly.*)

Step 2. Analyze the design. Analyze means you look for the way elements are related in a plan. Use the principles of design as a guide for analysis.

a. What kind of balance do you see? (*The left and right sides are similar. It has symmetrical balance.*)

b. What are the points of emphasis? (*The watery colors and shapes stand out.*)

c. Do you see normal or unusual proportions? (*You can't tell. Large shapes fill most of the picture.*)

d. Are patterns created by repeated elements? (*There are repeated elements but no strong pattern.*)

e. What elements give unity and variety to the design? (*The symmetrical design brings everything together. Variety comes from the blended colors and shapes.*)

f. Where do you see paths of movement or visual rhythms? (*Your eyes move up or down the center line and toward the borders.*)

Step 3. Interpret the artwork. Tell what you think and feel about the artwork.

a. State the causes or reasons for your ideas and feelings. (*The flowing colors and shapes make me feel everything is moving or changing. I think I see a butterfly or a flower. When I look again, I see a strange scene with melting shapes and colors.*)

b. Use phrases with adjectives and analogies. (*The center line is like a high ridge that makes watery colors flow down and out into a space. The colors blend into river-like shapes or lava flows. You might see a design like this in a dream or on another planet.*)

c. Think of a big idea or theme that helps to explain your ideas and feelings about the artwork. The meaning depends on the parts you notice. (*The title gives me this idea: People have the freedom to decide what the artwork means.*)

Step 4. Judge the artwork. Give a thoughtful and fair judgement. State your criteria, or standards, for judging the artwork. Then give reasons why the artwork meets, or does not meet, the criteria.

The criteria should fit the style or purpose of the artwork. For example, picture A is an abstract artwork. Only the design elements express ideas or feelings. How would you thoughtfully judge picture A? Do people always judge art in the same way? Why or why not?

What colors are trees? Many people say that trees are green with brownish trunks and branches. The paintings of trees in this lesson show that trees can have different colors. These artworks also show that artists can observe and interpret one **subject**, such as trees, in different ways.

The artists who created these **landscape** paintings worked outdoors. They set up their art materials so they could observe trees. They also let their own ideas and feelings become part of their work.

 Loren Mosley, *Dead Tree,* 1958. Oil on canvas, 28 x 22″ (71 x 56 cm). Valley House Gallery, Houston, Texas.

Loren Mosley's painting in picture A shows an outdoor scene in Texas. Most of the colors in this painting are mixtures of blue, green and violet. He mixed these **cool** colors with black and white to create many values. He used his brush to create many small patches of color.

What parts of the painting look like they came from observing the tree? Why might the artist have placed the tree in the center of the painting and made it so large that it fills the space? What other parts show the artist has interpreted the scene in his own way?

Tom Thomson, a Canadian artist, travelled deep into the wilderness to create paintings of forests and lakes. Most of the colors in picture B are **warm** mixtures of red, orange and yellow. Why do you think he used thick paint and large patches of color to suggest leaves? How has he captured a feeling of light and shadow?

You can combine observation and your own ideas in artworks. In this unit, you will learn more about ways to express your own ideas in art. You will also learn how artists develop their own styles of art.

Emil Nolde, *Daisies and Peonies.* Watercolor, 13 x 18 1/2" (33 x 47 cm). Edwin A. Ulrich Museum of Art, The Wichita State University (Endowment Association Art Collection).

The artworks in pictures A and B were created with transparent watercolor paints. **Transparent** means that you can see one color under another. Sometimes you can see the color and texture of the paper too. The thin, watery qualities of paint stand out in these two paintings.

Look at picture A. Emil Nolde is known as an **Expressionist** painter. He often used bright intense colors and bold brushstrokes to capture a feeling or idea. His painting is filled with the main shapes and colors of flowers. He added just a few details to suggest the petals and leaves.

Why do you think the flowers fill the whole **space**? Where do you see shapes or edges that look like brushstrokes? Where do you see colors that flow together?

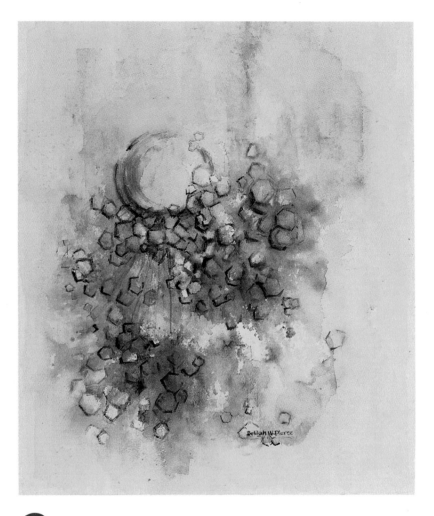

Painting tips

When you change colors, wash, wipe and blot the brush.

Paint the light colors and large areas first. For white, leave the paper unpainted.

Finish up with dark colors and details.

B **Delilah Pierce, *Nebulae,*** 1982. Watercolor, 29 x 22 1/2" (74 x 57 cm). Evans-Tibbs Gallery, Washington, DC.

Delilah Pierce, an African-American artist, explored many ideas in art. Her watercolor painting in picture B is done in an **Abstract** style. The colors are closely related. The shapes seem to float in space and pull toward the large circle. Do you know what the title means? It may help you interpret the painting.

You can explore the fluid, or flowing, qualities of watercolors. Use a sheet of paper for practice. Cut it in half. Wet one half and try different brushstrokes. Try some of the same brushstrokes on dry paper. How can you use these techniques in paintings?

After you have experimented, create a painting that has a special use of space. For example, the shapes and colors might float or pull in one main direction. The colors might suggest a closeup view of something you see or a distant place in outer space. Use your imagination.

Neutral Colors
Paintings With Earth Colors

Georgia O'Keeffe, *Grey Hills,* 1942. Oil on canvas, 20 x 30" (51 x 76 cm). ©1991 Indianapolis Museum of Art (Gift of Mr. and Mrs. James W. Fesler).

The two paintings in this lesson show colors of the earth. They also show the forms of land created by erosion.

Picture A shows hills in New Mexico. The artist, Georgia O'Keeffe, lived in New York City for many years but visited New Mexico during part of each year. She loved the colors and forms of the desert and hills of New Mexico. She later moved to New Mexico and created many paintings about the desert environment.

This painting has many neutral colors. **Neutral** colors are black, white and gray. Most artists also include brown as a neutral color. Neutral colors are not pure hues like you see on the color wheel.

Mixtures of white, black, gray and brown are often seen in nature. You also see neutral colors in many city buildings. Sometimes neutral colors look slightly **warm**, such as yellow-brown earth or red-brown bricks. Neutral colors can also look **cool**. A grayish blue metal and grayish green tree trunks are examples. Where do you see neutral colors in your environment?

Hale A. Woodruff, *Landscape*, 1936. Oil on canvas. Evans-Tibbs Gallery, Washington, DC.

Hale A. Woodruff, an African-American artist, created the painting in picture B while he was living and teaching art in Georgia. He was fascinated with the colors of the clay earth near Atlanta. His painting is dominated by warm-neutral colors. The dark contours, or edges, of forms make the land look rugged and bare. Why do you think these artists became interested in barren landscapes as subjects for artworks?

Practice mixing neutral colors that are light and dark, warm and cool. Many varieties of brown and gray can be mixed by combining yellow, red and blue.

Use your skill in mixing neutral colors to create a painting. Many animals, plants and views of places have subtle variations of neutral colors. What other subjects or moods might you express by using neutral colors?

A **Claudio Bravo,** *Still Life,* 1980. Pencil on paper, 14 1/4 x 20 5/8" (36 x 52 cm). Archer M. Huntington Art Gallery, The University of Texas at Austin (Barbara Duncan Fund, 1980). Photograph: George Holmes.

The artwork in picture A is a drawing of a still life. A **still life** is an artwork that shows objects. Many artists like the challenge of drawing a still life with different values. In art, **values** are differences in the lightness and darkness of colors. In many artworks, the main values are black, white and shades of gray.

This artist has shaded the forms to bring out the deep grooves and textures. You can see **shadows**, or dark values, on the right side of the forms. How has the artist shown where the light is coming from?

The still life drawing in picture B shows light and shadow on smooth forms. Where are the lightest and darkest values on these forms? How can you tell where the light is coming from? What are some visual clues that help you see the curved forms of the objects?

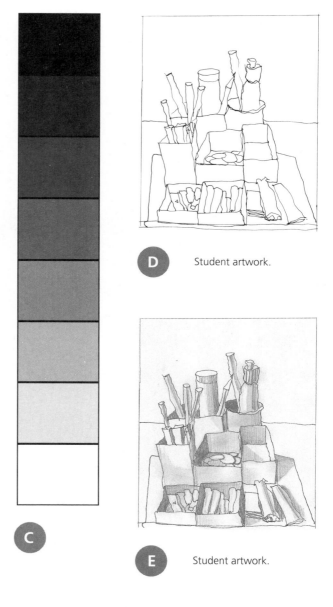

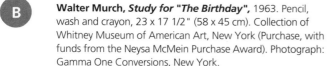

B **Walter Murch, *Study for "The Birthday"*,** 1963. Pencil, wash and crayon, 23 x 17 1/2 " (58 x 45 cm). Collection of Whitney Museum of American Art, New York (Purchase, with funds from the Neysa McMein Purchase Award). Photograph: Gamma One Conversions, New York.

C

D Student artwork.

E Student artwork.

You can develop your skill in seeing and drawing values by making a value scale. A **value scale** has white on one end and black on the other. The shades of gray between these ends gradually change from light to dark gray (see picture C).

Find and compose a still life of some objects. Choose objects that have special meaning to you, such as old shoes, musical instruments or sports equipment.

Draw the still life, then add shading to it. Picture D is a contour drawing created by a student. A **contour** drawing shows the edges or outlines of shapes. It is done very slowly and accurately. Picture E shows the same drawing after it was shaded.

Styles of Art
Painting a Still Life

William Harnett painted this still life about 100 years ago. The main subject is an old violin. What else do you see?

This style of art is one kind of **Realism**. The artist has used paint to create colors, textures and shapes that look real.

Henry Lee McFee created this painting about seventy years ago. The main subjects are books and fruit in a glass bowl.

The style of art is called **Cubism**. Notice how the artist used patches of paint to create shapes. The colors are not blended together. In some Cubist paintings, the colors of paint look like cubes and other geometric forms.

 B   **Henry Lee McFee, *Still Life,*** 1916. Oil on canvas, 20 x 16" (51 x 41 cm). Columbus Museum of Art, Ohio (Gift of Ferdinand Howald).

A   **William Harnett, *Old Models,*** 1892. Oil, 54 x 28" (138 x 71 cm). Museum of Fine Arts, Boston (The Hayden Collection).

Roy Lichtenstein, *Still Life with Crystal Bowl,* 1973. Oil and synthetic polymer on canvas, 52 x 42" (132 x 107 cm). Collection of Whitney Museum of American Art, New York (Purchase, with funds from Frances and Sydney Lewis). Photograph: Geoffrey Clements.

Roy Lichtenstein created this painting about twenty years ago. This style of painting is called Pop art. Pop is a short word for popular. **Pop art** usually tells about things you see in stores or advertisements.

Create a painting of a still life. Paint it in your own **style**. The steps in picture D will help you learn to paint efficiently. An efficient artist works quickly and thoughtfully.

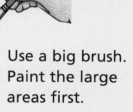

Use a big brush. Paint the large areas first.

If shapes are the same color, paint them next.

Add light, dark and related colors.

Use a small brush to add details.

The art of Asia includes many countries and traditions in art. The paintings in this lesson were created by a Korean artist over 100 years ago. The paintings were mounted on **folding screens**. The screens were used to decorate rooms and to help keep them warm.

Each painting is designed around a long line that looks like an S or a Z. The animals are placed just above or below the center of the painting. The writing at the top is a brief poem or phrase about the painting. This kind of informal or **asymmetrical** design is often found in Asian art.

The plants and small animals in these paintings are **symbols** for ideas. The symbols are explained on the next page.

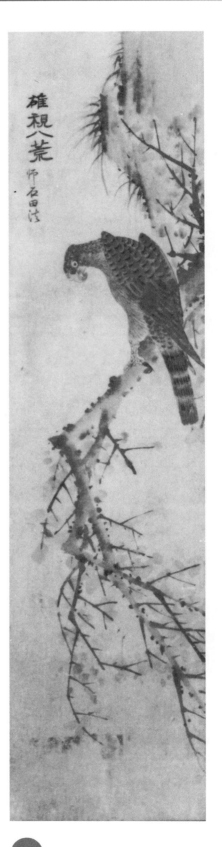

Picture A: Cranes are spiritual messengers. Pine trees stay green through many years. They are symbols of hope for a long life.

Picture B: Hawks are guardians. They fly high and have keen eyes to watch for danger.

Picture C: Magpies are messengers who bring good news to villagers. The plum tree blossoms are a symbol for spring.

Picture D: A carp (or salmon) swims upstream and leaps rapids to reach the place where it spawns. It is a symbol for courage and dedication.

Plants and animals are symbols for ideas in many cultures. Find out more about natural symbols in art. Then create a painting using your own ideas and symbols from nature. You might plan the painting around design principles used in Asian screen paintings.

Hwacho (Birds and Flowers), Yi Dynasty, 19th century, 4 panels from a 10-panel screen painting, ink and color on linen, 47 3/4 x 11 3/4" (121 x 30 cm). The Brooklyn Museum, New York (Collection: Mary Ann Durgin).

C

D

21 Symbols from Nature
A Monoprint Project

 Linda Lomahaftewa, *Cloud Maiden Series #13*, 1988. Monoprint with oil pastels, 22 x 30" (56 x 76 cm). Courtesy of the artist.

Monoprints similar to picture A are made in several steps. In a **monoprint**, you create only one print. (Mono means one.) To begin, you put printer's ink over a smooth surface, such as metal or plastic. You apply the ink with a **brayer**, or small roller covered with rubber.

While the ink is wet, you wipe away some of the ink with tools, such as a cotton swab, sponge or the edge of cardboard.

You can also press paper shapes on top of the ink to make designs. The moon and cross-like shapes in this print may have been cut from paper.

When the design is complete, you place paper over the wet ink and rub it. This transfers the ink to the paper. When you lift the paper, the print is completed.

This artist drew on top of the dry ink to create other textures and lines. Where do you see the added textures and lines?

Doves are symbols for peace. They fly in the heavens and inspire thoughts of purity and hope in people.
Leroy Johnson   gr. 5

Student artwork.

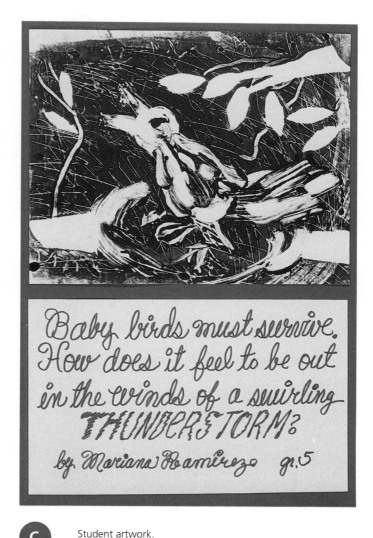

Baby birds must survive. How does it feel to be out in the winds of a swirling THUNDERSTORM?
by Mariana Ramirez   gr. 5

Student artwork.

Look again at picture A. From the title, you can tell that it shows a woman. The woman is a symbol for a cloud or sky spirit who brings rain. The artist is a North American Indian who makes art about her Hopi and Choctaw heritage. Her ancestors helped her learn stories about the cloud maiden and other Indian symbols for nature. Why are the sky, clouds and rain important visual symbols for nature?

Students created the monoprints in pictures B and C. Their class explored ideas about nature. They did research to learn about birds as symbols in art. They also expressed their own ideas and feelings about birds. They created a display of their work.

Think of a related project that your class can do. Research the topic and create a display or book with monoprints as illustrations.

Vincent van Gogh, *Sunflowers,* 1887. Oil on canvas, 24 x 17" (61 x 43 cm). The Metropolitan Museum of Art, New York (Rogers Fund).

The artworks in this lesson have the same basic subject. Each artist has observed and expressed ideas about flowers in a closeup view. In a **closeup** view, a picture space is filled with one or several main shapes.

Vincent van Gogh created several paintings of sunflowers. Notice the rough textures and angular edges of the petals. The center of the flower has no seeds. Both of the flowers look dry, brittle and withered. Some people say the flowers are symbols for autumn and the process of aging. Can you think of other ways to interpret the painting?

Now look at the painting by Lowell Nesbitt in picture B. It shows an iris, a very delicate flower. The forms have been shaded to look like sculpture. The petals swirl and fold in many directions. An **art critic** said that Lowell Nesbitt's flowers look like "cosmic forces moving toward you from outer space." Can you think of other interpretations of *Blue Iris*?

 Lowell Nesbitt, *Blue Iris,* 1981. Oil on canvas. Courtesy of the artist.

 Georgia O'Keeffe, *Red Canna,* ca.1923. Oil on canvas mounted on masonite, 36 x 29 7/8" (91 x 76 cm). Collection of the University of Arizona Museum of Art, Tucson (Gift of Oliver James).

In the painting by Georgia O'Keeffe, a detail of a large canna flower fills the space. The petals ripple upward and outward from the bottom of the painting. The colors and shapes blend together. Some people say that petals of canna flowers remind them of flames.

What other design qualities did each artist want you to see? How do these paintings differ from **scientific illustrations** of flowers?

Find a flower, leaf, twig or other form in nature. Make some sketches of it. Think about the ideas or feelings you can communicate about it.

For example, some twigs may remind you of old, knobby fingers on a hand. Others may remind you of a strong, muscular arm. While you are sketching, try to bring out, or emphasize, the way your natural form can be a symbol for an idea or feeling. Develop your best ideas into a finished artwork.

55

 Franz Marc, *The Large Blue Horses,* 1911. Oil on canvas, 41 5/16 x 71 1/4" (105 x 181 cm). Collection, Walker Art Center, Minneapolis (Gift of the T. B. Walker Foundation, Gilbert M. Walker Fund, 1942).

Have you ever seen blue horses or dogs that are pink, violet and green? Why do you think artists might use colors such as these?

Artists who create paintings have always been fascinated with color. About eighty years ago in Europe, artists began to explore how colors could be used to express feelings. These artists became leaders of a style called **Expressionism**.

Franz Marc's painting is an example of this style. He created many paintings of animals with unusual colors. He thought that animals were noble and beautiful. He used colors to suggest the inner spirit of each kind of animal.

In many Expressionist artworks, bold colors and simple shapes work together. For example, in this painting, the artist uses many curved forms to create gentle flowing rhythms across the whole painting. What other visual elements help to express a special mood or feeling?

Robin Eschner, *Sally Always Wondered Whether She Was Adopted.* Watercolor. ©1990 Allport Editions Greeting Cards.

Today, many artists use unusual colors to express ideas and feelings. They also use colors to get your attention and make you think.

Robin Eschner's painting in picture B has colors that get your attention and make you think. The dogs look **realistic** except for the colors of three dogs. Read the title of the painting. How does it make you think about the painting?

Think about animals that have special meaning to you. Then think about colors that seem to go with your feelings about the animals. Make some sketches of your ideas. Then create an artwork using colors to express a definite mood.

A student created the painting in picture C. He chose colors to express his fear of scorpions. Do you think the painting is an example of Expressionism? Why or why not?

C Student artwork.

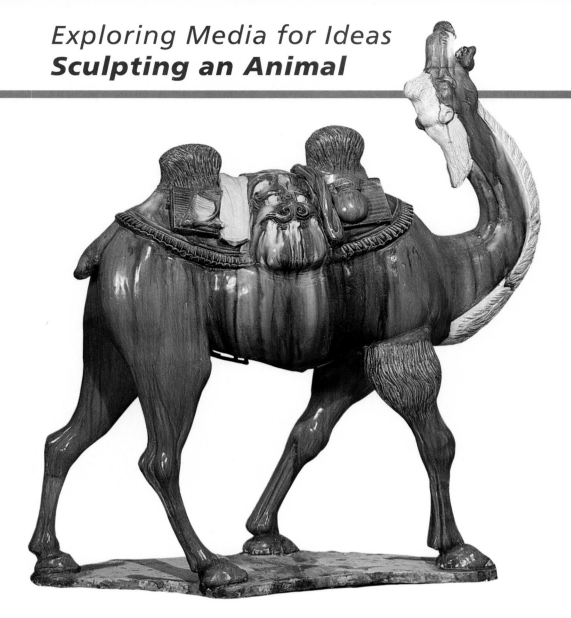

 Camel, China, T'ang Dynasty. Glazed and colored clay, 34 3/4 x 29 1/2" (88 x 75 cm). Los Angeles County Museum of Art (The William Randolph Hearst Collection).

Most of your artwork has been flat or **two-dimensional**. In this lesson you will create a sculpture. A sculpture is **three-dimensional**. It has height, width and depth, or thickness.

These two sculptures suggest movement. You get this feeling because parts, such as the neck, head and legs, bend. Some artists say sculptures like these show "frozen movement." What do you think this means?

Movement is **obvious**, or easy to see, in the camel. The neck curves back. The head stretches up. The legs slant and bend.

In China, camels were valued as symbols of wealth. This camel is made from **ceramic** clay, a moist earth. After the form was modeled, the clay was allowed to dry. The dry sculpture was **fired**, or baked, in a kiln to make the clay stronger and more permanent. A **kiln** is like a furnace or oven.

The artist finished the sculpture with glaze. **Glaze** is a mixture of water and colored minerals. When the glazed work is fired again, the minerals melt and create a glassy coating.

Rosa Bonheur, *Grazing Ewe,* ca. 1846. Bronze, 6 x 4 x 8 1/2 " (15 x 10 x 22 cm). The Fine Arts Museum of San Francisco (Gift of Archer M. Huntington).

The sculpture of the grazing sheep has a **subtle** movement. The neck and head move down in a diagonal or slanting direction. The diagonal bends in the legs help to suggest a walking motion. How did the artist show the texture of the sheep?

Create a sculpture of an animal. You might begin with parts and put them together firmly. Try to show an obvious or a subtle **movement**. You might choose an animal as a symbol for an idea or feeling. What texture will your sculpture have?

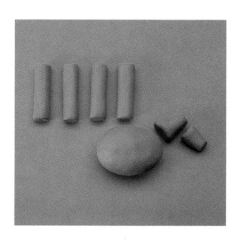

Erich Heckel, *Head of a Girl,* 1912. Pencil on paper, 17 5/8 x 13 1/4" (45 x 34 cm). Sheldon Memorial Art Gallery, University of Nebraska-Lincoln (F.M. Hall Collection).

Ramón Gómez Cornet, *Head of a Boy,* 1942. Oil on canvas, 21 7/8 x 17 3/8" (56 x 44 cm). Collection, The Museum of Modern Art, New York (Inter-American Fund).

What is the first thing that you notice about the four artworks in this lesson? Can you find the main similarities?

All of these artworks are portraits. A **portrait** shows a likeness of a person. These portraits have a similar **theme**. All of them show people who are thinking.

Practice looking at these portraits as experts do. Experts look at artworks carefully. They combine seeing, thinking and imagining. These are skills that help you get a feeling about an artwork.

Choose one of the portraits. Imagine that you can be that person. As you look at the portrait, try to take the same **pose.** Try to imagine exactly how the person feels and what they are thinking about.

Now imagine you are the artist who created the portrait. Imagine how you would plan the artwork. Imagine you are creating all of the edges, textures and other details.

Lev T. Mills, *Gemini I,* 1969. Etching. Evans-Tibbs Gallery, Washington, DC.

Fernand Leger, *Face and Hands,* 1952. Brush and ink, 26 x 19 3/4" (66 x 50 cm). Collection, The Museum of Modern Art, New York (Mrs. Wendell T. Bush Fund).

Compare the moods and expressions in each portrait. How do the positions of the hands differ? Where do the eyes seem to be looking? Are the heads, necks and shoulders in the same positions?

Each of the artists has used a different **medium**, or set of materials, to create a portrait. Can you tell how these materials, or **media**, made each work look special?

Ask a classmate or someone at home to pose while you draw them. Have them pose so one or both of their hands are near the face.

Create your portrait in pencil, marker or another medium you like to use. You might prefer to combine several media such as marker with crayon.

 John La Farge, *Portrait of a Young Boy,* 1860–1862. Oil on canvas, 21 x 16" (53 x 41 cm). Denver Art Museum, Colorado (Helen Dill Collection).

B **Laura Wheeler Waring, *Anna Washington Derry,*** 1927. Oil on canvas, 20 x 16" (51 x 41 cm). National Museum of American Art, Smithsonian Institution, Washington, DC (Gift of the Harmon Foundation)/Art Resource, New York.

In this lesson, you see three portraits by adult artists and one created by a student your age. You can see similarities and differences in the poses and moods of each portrait.

What is the first thing you notice about John La Farge's portrait in picture A? Does the boy seem to be looking at you? Why? Where has the artist created shading on the face, hair, neck and body? How does the artist use paint to show the **shadows**?

Laura Wheeler Waring was an African-American artist who created many portraits to honor the memory of people. Her painting in picture A shows a woman in a relaxed pose. What expression does her face have? What kind of shading has the artist used? Where?

Compare the **lighting** in these two paintings. Can you tell exactly where the light might be coming from? How does each artist use paint to create shadows and highlights? A **highlight** is a very light area on a surface.

Robert Henri, _Gregorita with the Santa Clara Bowl,_ 1917. Oil on canvas, 32 x 26" (81 x 66 cm). Edwin A. Ulrich Museum of Art, The Wichita State University (Endowment Association Art Collection).

D Student artwork.

Robert Henri was an American artist who created portraits and other paintings about real life. This portrait shows a Pueblo Indian girl with a large clay bowl from the Santa Clara Pueblo in New Mexico. Where do you see shadows and highlights?

A student created the portrait in picture D. The changes in value, or light and dark colors, help you to see the forms of the face, neck and hair. What other techniques of using paint did he use?

Choose one of your sketches of a person or a drawing of yourself. Create a portrait using paint. Mix tints and shades of colors to show the form of the nose, eyes and other features.

Begin with one color for all the skin. Then add highlights, or light colors, to show the forms that stand out, such as the nose, cheeks, chin and forehead. Add slightly darker colors to show the shadows and details. Can you explain why these steps can help you?

Planning an Artwork
Capturing Moods of People

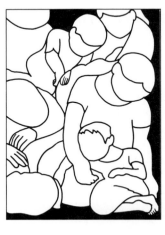

A Diego Rivera, *Sleep,* 1932. Lithograph, 16 1/4 x 11 1/8"
(41 x 28 cm). The Metropolitan Museum of Art, New York
(Harris Brisbane Dick Fund, 1933).

B

C

The artworks in pictures A and D show two very different moods of people. Let's look at the way the plan, or design, helps to express the different moods.

The drawing *Sleep* was created by Mexican artist Diego Rivera. The artist shows farm workers who are tired and asleep in a crowded space. Have you ever been as tired and sleepy as these people look?

Study the design in *Sleep*. The main lines and shapes create a path of movement. Look for gentle curves that slump or sway downward (see diagram B).

The figures are grouped together and fill most of the space. The space filled with the figures is called **positive** space because you notice it first. The **negative** space is the background. You notice negative space after you see the positive space (see diagram C).

Now look at Martin Fletcher's painting in picture D. It is designed to show the excitement of a boxing match. The winner and his helper are leaping. The announcer and photographer are also shown with

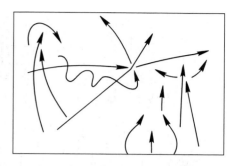

Fletcher Martin, *The Glory,* 1949. Oil on canvas, 34 x 48" (86 x 122 cm). Edwin A. Ulrich Museum of Art, The Wichita State University (Gift of Mr. and Mrs. Robert Blauner).

lines and shapes that move up, out or around (see diagram E). Why do these paths of movement create a feeling of energy and excitement?

The largest figures in *The Glory* fill much of the space in the picture. Notice how the positive and negative spaces curve, twist and turn. Why do you think the artist planned the space in this way? (See diagram F.)

Plan an artwork with several people in a space. Think about a definite feeling or idea to express. How could you express ideas or moods such as hope, courage, pity or boredom? Make up a short title for your work and keep it in mind while you are planning the picture.

Lightly sketch some of the "action" lines, or paths of movement, that go with the title you have chosen. Then draw the main figures so the arms, legs and other parts of the body are close to the action lines. How will you plan the positive and negative spaces in your work?

Elaine de Kooning, *Scrimmage,* 1953. Oil on canvas, 25 x 36" (64 x 91 cm). Albright-Knox Art Gallery, Buffalo, New York (Gift of Mr. and Mrs. David K. Anderson to the Martha Jackson Collection, 1974).

There are many ways to suggest the motion of people in an artwork. Let's look at the **techniques**, or methods, that two artists used.

Elaine de Kooning works in a style called **Abstract Expressionism**. In this style, the artist abstracts, or leaves out details and captures the main idea or feeling in a subject. The painter also moves the brush in a way that matches a feeling the artist wants to express.

In many ways, this painting is like a quick sketch. The artist quickly brushed in the action lines and colors for each figure, without any details. Then she used similar **brushstrokes** to fill the background and outline some of the figures. The blurred and choppy edges of the shapes help to capture the feeling of rapid, colliding motion.

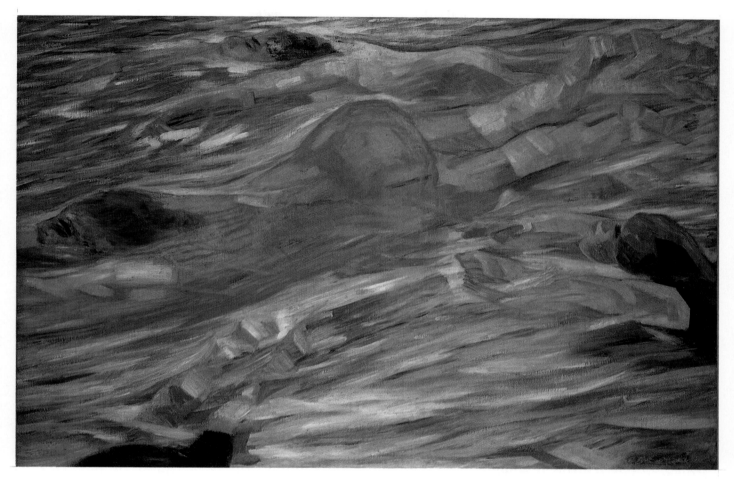

Carlo Carrá, *The Swimmers,* 1910. Oil on canvas, 41 7/16 x 61 1/4" (105 x 156 cm).
The Carnegie Museum of Art, Pittsburgh (Gift of G. David Thompson).
Photograph: Kevin Brunelle.

Some of the same techniques are used in *The Swimmers* by Carlo Carrá. He was a leader in the style known as **Futurism**. These artists thought motion and energy were important ideas for present and future art. They explored ways to show the motion and energy of people, animals, machines and other subjects.

This artist has used a wide brush and subtle changes in color. The diagonal brushstrokes show the flowing motion of water and gliding action of the swimmers. What else creates the illusion of motion?

Choose an activity or sport where people move quickly, smoothly, or in some other special way. Create a painting by making some **gestures** in the air like the motions you want to show. As you begin painting, use similar brushstrokes to fill in a background and show the figures. What else can you do?

A

B

C

Have you ever watched an artist create a large complex painting? How do artists plan their work and develop it?

Artists do not work in exactly the same way, but they do learn from each other. The photographs in pictures A, B, C and D show a few steps that one artist used. What can you learn from this artist's technique, or method, of painting?

Jacob Lawrence is an African-American painter who has received many honors. In 1973, he was invited to create paintings about George Washington Bush, an African-American pioneer who led people over the Oregon Trail to the west coast of the United States.

Notice how the artist began with a sketch of all the basic shapes. In picture B, you see that he began painting some of the larger background shapes. When he mixed a color, he applied it to more than one area of the painting.

In picture C, most of the largest shapes are completed. In picture D, many details have been added. If you compare pictures D and E, you can find some of the last things added to the painting. What are they? Why might he wait so long to add them?

Jacob Lawrence became interested in African-American history when he was thirteen. His first major project was a series of forty-one paintings about the quest for freedom by the slaves in Haiti.

What topics do you like to study? Choose one and develop a painting about it. How will you plan and work on your painting?

Jacob Lawrence, *George Washington Bush Series,* 1973. *Panel 2: In the Iowa Territory, they rendez-voused with a wagon train headed for the Oregon Trail.* Five stages: a) drawing, graphite on gessoed paperboard, b) stage 1, c) stage 2, d) stage 3, e) final stage. Casein-gouache on paperboard, 31 1/2 x 19 1/2 " (80 x 49 cm). Photograph: Paul Macapia.

  Ichiryusai Hiroshige, *Ohashi, Sudden Shower at Atake (Storm on the Great Bridge),* 1857. Woodcut, 13 x 11 11/16" (33 x 30 cm). The Toledo Museum of Art, Toledo, Ohio (Carrie L. Brown Bequest Fund).

Printmaking is one way artists express what they see, think and feel. The artworks in pictures A and B are **woodcuts**. The artists carved lines and shapes into blocks of wood. Then they put thick ink on the block and pressed paper against the ink. This process allows the artist to create many copies of an artwork from the same woodcut.

Compare the styles of the prints. How has each artist expressed special ideas about a bridge? Where do you see evidence of different times and cultures in the artworks?

Clare Romano, *Bridge in the City II.* 1962. Woodcut, sheet: 28 13/16 x 16 9/16" (73 x 42 cm); image: 23 x 13 1/4" (58 x 34 cm). Collection of Whitney Museum of American Art, New York (Gift of Rock-Hil-Uris, Inc.).

Sketch ideas for a print. Your print will be made from a block of Styrofoam. Trace the edges of your block on paper several times. This will help you make sketches the same size as the block.

Put your best sketch on the block and re-draw the lines, pressing thin lines into the block.

Remove your drawing. Continue pressing your pencil into the Styrofoam. Your lines and shapes should look as if they are carved into the block. To print your block, follow the steps in picture C.

Roll ink onto the brayer. Roll the inked brayer across the block.

Place paper over the block.
Rub the paper to press the ink onto it.
Carefully lift the paper.
This step is called pulling the print.

C

D Student artwork.

E Student artwork.

A student made the prints in pictures D and E. She made the prints by putting ink on her Styrofoam carving. Study your first prints. You may want to change parts of your block as she did. Can you find the differences in pictures D and E?

Put your name and a title on your prints. Keep and mount the best ones.

 Vincent van Gogh, *The Starry Night,* 1889. Oil on canvas, 29 x 36 1/4" (73 x 92 cm). Collection, The Museum of Modern Art, New York (Acquired through the Lillie P. Bliss Bequest).

In this lesson, you can show what you have learned about looking at art. Then show what you have learned about creating art.

Both of the paintings in this lesson are filled with rhythmic movements. You have learned that a visual rhythm can remind you of a dance. Sometimes visual rhythms have a definite beat, like the rhythms in music.

Look at *The Starry Night*. Vincent van Gogh was a Dutch painter who led others to explore how colors and brushstrokes can

express strong feelings. His work is done in a style called **Expressionism**.

Where do you see visual rhythms in this painting? What elements of design are repeated in the painting? For example, curves make swirls and circles in the sky. Where else do you see many curves? What feeling do they help to create? What else can you describe, analyze and interpret?

B Joseph Stella, *Luna Park,* ca. 1913. Oil on composition board, 17 1/2 x 23 3/8" (45 x 59 cm). Collection of Whitney Museum of American Art, New York (Gift of Mrs. Charles A. Goldberg). Photograph: Geoffrey Clements.

Joseph Stella's painting in picture B also has a feeling of great energy and motion. This painting is also Expressionist in style. It captures the sparkling activity of an amusement park.

The visual rhythms in this painting come from repeated lines, shapes and colors. What other design elements can you describe? What design principles did the artist use? What are the main similarities and differences in the two paintings?

See if you can create an artwork with visual rhythms. Try to capture a feeling of light, energy and motion at night. Do not copy the artworks in this lesson. Use different ideas. You might show the tracer lights from rocket ships in space. You might show colorful lights that glide or swirl at nighttime festivals. What other ideas can you explore?

Art in Your World
Living with Art, Past and Present

Have you ever thought about becoming an architect, sculptor or painter? Do you like to build models or write about art? Do you have other interests and skills for an **art career**?

There are hundreds of art careers. Today, people with art training help to design almost everything you see, buy or use. They also plan the buildings in your community.

Special schools and programs help artists prepare for art careers. For example, in picture A, a student in an art school is learning about **interior design**. Can you explain why she has created drawings and a model of the interior?

In picture B, the artist is explaining how he used a computer to create an illustration. The **illustration** is similar to cartoons in motion pictures and television. Do you know how a computer can help artists do other kinds of artwork?

Artists design many images that give you information or entertain you. What art skills are needed to create motion pictures, television and other images that communicate to many people?

Troy A. Gerth at computer.

C Interior, Museum of Anthropology,
University of British Columbia.

D Elizabeth Catlett in her studio.

In many art careers, people help others to appreciate and understand art. The museum in picture C has many art workers. **Docents** help visitors understand and see the art. **Curators** do research and help to decide what to display.

Conservators study ways to protect the rare and old artworks from decay and damage. Can you think of other careers that help people see and learn about art?

Have you ever visited the **studio**, or workplace, of an artist? In picture D, you see Elizabeth Catlett's sculpture studio. The studio is set up so she can do carvings and work in other media. She works in her own way. Her best work is shown in an art gallery or an art museum.

In this unit, you will learn more about art careers and kinds of art that many people use or see. If you could choose an art career, what would you like to do? Why? How can you find out more about careers in art?

Architecture is the art and science of planning buildings. Architects study types and styles of buildings from the past. Look at these styles of houses created from colonial times to the present. Compare and contrast the roofs, doors and other details. Have you seen similar house fronts, or **facades**?

Imagine a dream house of your own. Draw a picture that shows how the facade might look.

1620   Frame house with thatched roof, stick and mud chimney.

1830   Gothic house with many pointed arches.

1855   Mansard house with rooms on the third floor.

1920   California Mission house with tile roof.

1950   Ranch house with large picture window in front.

Drawings from *Environmental Interiors* by Weale, Croake and Weale. Macmillan Publishing Co., 1982. Used by permission. Mary Jo Weale and Tim J. Bookout.

1690 Cape Cod house with one chimney for the entire house.

1770 Salt-box house with two stories, attic, one chimney.

1900 The Craftsman house with concrete on the front.

1905 Bungalow with wood shingle roof.

1980 Modern house with windows of different sizes and shapes, stained wood finish.

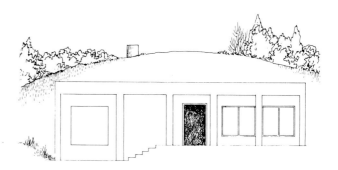

1990 Energy-saving house set in a hill to help keep the house cool in summer and warm in winter.

Architecture on the Outside
Materials for Buildings

B Country villa of Frederic Church, ca. 1870. Olana, New York Historic Site. ©Friends of Olana, Inc.

A Courtesy of T. Ritchie Architects, Inc., Toronto, Canada.

Architects think about the materials they want in a building. They think about the colors, textures and patterns of materials on the **exterior**, or outside.

Many large buildings today are constructed of steel, concrete and glass. Steel and glass are smooth. Concrete can be finished to look smooth or rough. What colors and textures have you seen in building materials?

Bricks are made of clay. They are often used for homes. Most bricks have a warm color. Frederick Church's house in picture B has many shades of bricks. It also has some designs made from glazed clay tiles.

Frederick Church was a well-known painter in America. He traveled to many lands. He used architectural ideas from buildings he saw in Europe and Asia.

 Studio House in Woodstock, New York, 1986. R.M. Kliment & Frances Halsband Architects. Photograph: Cervin Robinson, ©1991.

 Donald Rokoski, architectural rendering.

Frances Halsband is a well-known architect. She has designed many kinds of buildings. She has also created plans for improving New York City and Pasadena, California. She helped design the artist's studio in picture C.

The studio has **natural stone** at the bottom. These stones came from nearby hills. The top part of the house and the roof have overlapped shingles. **Shingles** are thin boards with deep grooves that drain water away from the house. What other materials did the architect use?

Architects must also choose materials in relation to their cost and the way they conserve energy. What are some common materials for buildings in your town? Why are they used so often?

Sketch patterns and textures you see in different buildings. Find out why certain materials are used on the exterior of homes, schools and other kinds of buildings.

Show what you have learned by creating an architectural illustration. Try to show the textures and patterns of materials in a building. The drawing in picture D was made by a college student. He is preparing for a career as an **illustrator**.

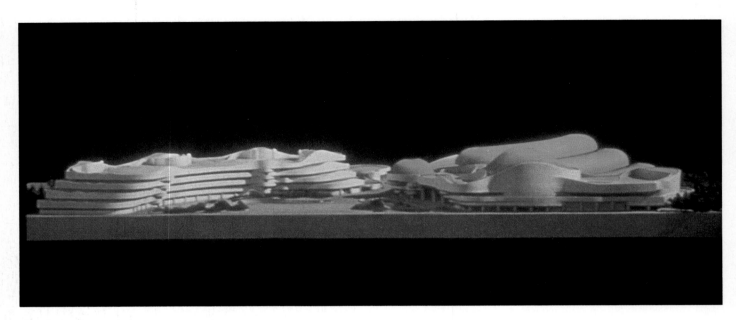

Douglas Cardinal, *Model for the Canadian Museum of Civilization*. Courtesy of Douglas Cardinal Architect, Canada.

Douglas Cardinal designed the Canadian museum in picture A. The design has many organic, or curved, forms. **Organic** forms are similar to forms in nature. The curves in this building move up, down and around. The whole building is unified by the graceful flow of curves. **Unity** means all of the parts work together, like a team.

Many architects of the twentieth century have designed buildings with unusual curves. They are interested in the beauty of curved forms in nature. They have also designed buildings with flowing rhythms that make the buildings look like sculpture.

Antonio Gaudi's architecture in picture B has many curved forms. The forms and details in his building are based on nature. The curves are similar to vines and other plants with graceful curves. The curved rhythms help to unify the building. What other elements help to unify it?

Antonio Gaudi, *Casa Mila,* 1905–07, Barcelona, Spain. Photograph: F. Arborio, Milan.

 Felix Candela, *Church of La Florida,* Mexico City, ca. 1950. Courtesy of George Barford.

 Frank Lloyd Wright, *Exterior of Solomon R. Guggenheim Museum,* 1956–59, New York.

Look at the wavy rhythms and curves of the building in picture C. Do they remind you of the curved forms in a clam shell? Do they remind you of the repeated flowing forms in a flower? If you walked inside this building, what would the spaces be like?

 Le Corbusier, *The Chapel of Notre-Dame-du-Haut,* 1951–55, Ronchamp, France. Photograph: P.H. Beighton.

Le Corbusier was interested in sculpture and architecture. Look at picture D. How are the forms in this chapel similar to a sculpture made of clay? How might forms like these be made in concrete?

Frank Lloyd Wright was one of America's most inventive architects. He designed the art museum in picture E. The museum is in New York City. Do the curves in this building remind you of forms in a shell?

Today, architects can use concrete, steel and other materials to create buildings with unusual forms and spaces. Are there some buildings with many curved rhythmic forms in your town?

A student used clay to create the architectural model in picture F. Explore ideas for a model of your own. Your building might have forms similar to a shell, bird, fish or flower. What other forms in nature could you explore for an architectural model? How can you unify your design?

Many people create interior designs. They want to choose or arrange furniture so it looks attractive and fits their way of life.

The four rooms you see here are in museums. The rooms are **replicas**, or models, of actual interiors in North American homes. Each room has a special look or style. You can see the changes in styles by comparing details, such as the shapes of chairs and designs of rugs.

In picture A, you see an **Early Colonial** home. Colonists, or early settlers from Europe, designed and hand-crafted almost every item in the room.

Between 1700 and 1800, cities grew in size. Many had factories and stores. Wealthy people could buy their furniture, dishes and many items to decorate their homes. They could also buy things from other lands.

The room in picture B has design ideas from many nations. The designs for the wallpaper, folding screen and ceramics came from China. The designs for chairs came from England and France. This combination of design ideas became popular for homes of wealthy people.

Chinese Parlor, ca. 1875. Museum installation. Courtesy of Winterthur Museum, Delaware.

Interior of Plymton House, New England, 17th century. From the Collections of Henry Ford Museum & Greenfield Village.

Between 1800 and 1900, many artists travelled to Europe and other lands. They brought back design ideas for people to use in their homes. These artists were the first interior designers. An **interior designer** helps people to plan the interior, or inside spaces, of a building.

The room in picture C has many design ideas from France. The fancy style, called **Rococo**, was a favorite of French kings and queens. Why might wealthy Americans have wanted homes and furniture in this style?

Today, many people still like design ideas from the past. The room in picture D has many designs from the Colonial period. Yet, almost every object in this room has been manufactured in the last twenty years! Why do you think some people like these designs?

Do some research on interior design. Find out about different styles and types of furniture. Learn about other decisions an interior designer makes. Design a room in which you would like to live.

 Parlor from Colonel Robert J. Milligan House, Saratoga Springs, New York. 1853. Museum installation. The Brooklyn Museum, New York (Gift of Sarah Milligan Rand, Kate Milligan Brill and the Dick S. Ramsay Fund).

 Knob Creek, North Carolina, 1980. Gallery installation. Bucks County Collection.

Rock gardens of the Daisen-in, Daitoku-Ji, ca. 1509. Kyoto, Japan.

Have you ever heard of a "dry garden?" The garden in picture A is a well-known dry garden. It was designed about 500 years ago by a religious leader in Japan. Many dry gardens are designed to look like a **miniature**, or very small, landscape.

The small pebbles are symbols for water. The small pond is a symbol for the ocean. What do you think the larger rocks might be symbols for? Gardens like this are created to help people think about the subtle beauty of large and small things in nature. The gardens are not entered, but seen as if they are paintings.

Have you ever wondered why many people enjoy park-like spaces? The park-like space in picture B is in downtown Baltimore, Maryland.

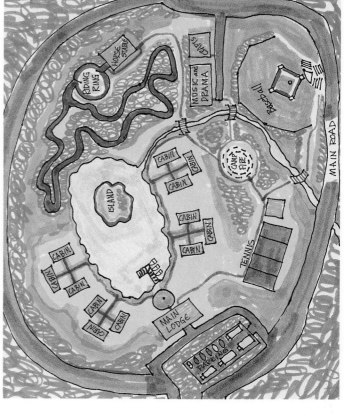

B   **Eberhard H. Zeidler,** *The Gallery at Harborplace,* 1981. Baltimore, Maryland. Exterior waterfall. Zeidler Roberts Partnership, Architects. Photograph: Balthazar Korab.

C   Student artwork.

Many people who live in cities want land to be saved for parks. Even small parks with gardens add beauty to a city. The natural environment adds variety and interest to a city. What are some of the best parks or gardens in or near your city? Why are they "the best"?

Some artists are **landscape architects**. They create plans for outdoor spaces such as parks, gardens and recreation areas. Some landscape architects design zoos and amusement parks.

Students worked together on the design for a camp in picture C. Their drawing shows a "bird's eye" view of the camp. They used yellow-green to show lawns. A middle-green shows low bushes. Tall trees are dark green loops. What else is clearly shown in the plan?

 George Sugarman, *Kite Castle,* 1973. Painted steel, 18′ (5.5 m). Hammarskjold Plaza, New York. Courtesy of Robert Miller Gallery, New York.

B **Alexander Calder,** *Stegosaurus.* Steel plate, 50′ (15.2 m). Burt McManus Memorial Plaza, Hartford, Connecticut.

Today artists can create large outdoor sculptures from sheets or tubes of metal. The pieces of metal are cut out, bent and welded together. Many people may help **assemble** the sculpture. Sometimes cranes are used to lift very heavy parts.

George Sugarman designed the sculpture in picture A for a plaza in New York City. The steel has been painted different colors. The sculpture is 18 feet (5.5 m) tall.

Artists must carefully plan a very large sculpture. This planning is done by creating a **model** of the sculpture. The model helps them try out ideas and solve problems. The model helps them see how the sculpture will look from all sides.

Alexander Calder designed the sculpture in picture B for a plaza in Hartford, Connecticut. Can you imagine how a small paper model could be used to plan this steel sculpture? The finished sculpture is 50 feet (15 m) tall.

C

curl

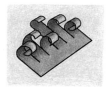
fringe

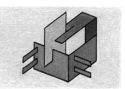
slot and join

fold

slit

D

score and bend

E

Canadian artist Colette Whiten prepared the model you see in picture C. She made it for an art competition for a park. Her idea was chosen. Her completed sculpture is shown in picture D. Her puzzle-like design uses positive and negative shapes as a main idea. Her design also invites people to compare their height to the height of the figures in the sculptures.

You can create a model for a large sculpture. Imagine that your sculpture could be made from steel or other strong materials. Imagine it will be a sculpture for a park or plaza. Picture E shows some ways to use paper to create a three-dimensional form. What kind of outdoor sculpture will you design?

B   Vancouver Government Center, British Columbia, 1979. Design: Arthur Erickson Associates.

A   Ghirardelli Square, San Francisco, 1983–87. Benjamin Thompson Associates. Photograph: Fred Lyon.

There are many kinds of art. People with special art skills planned the San Francisco business district in picture A. **Architects** planned the main buildings and spaces around them. Some architects specialize in urban, or city, design. An urban designer coordinates very large projects like this one.

A **sculptor** made the figures for the fountain. **Industrial designers** planned the benches, lamps and many products sold in the stores. Can you find other kinds of art in this scene?

The new civic center in picture B was designed by Canadian Arthur Erickson. The whole structure is designed to bring beauty and excitement to the city. There are several waterfalls and many small, park-like spaces in the center. The steps let people see the spectacular center from many angles.

Jane Thompson, *Revitalized Interior, Union Station*, Washington, DC, 1984–88. Courtesy of Steve Rosenthall Architectural Photography.

Picture C shows the redesigned interior of an old train station in Washington, DC. The plan was developed by urban designer Jane Thompson. She has helped people in Boston, San Francisco, New York and St. Paul redesign old parts of their cities. She has worked on similar projects in Australia and Europe.

Do you see the Greek columns in this train station? They are part of the old interior. What parts of the interior look newer? How do the newer parts make the space attractive and helpful to people?

Many artists and architects today want to make cities better places for all people. They work out plans to restore beauty and comfort to city life. They plan buildings and spaces that are practical for residents of a city and attractive to visitors.

What parts of your town are attractive or beautiful? What improvements would you like to see? Why? Draw a picture or plan. Show an attractive part of your town, or draw a plan for improving an area of it.

Utility vehicle. Injection molding, blow molding, compression molding. Courtesy of General Electric Plastics.

B **Lange Freestyle ice skates.** Courtesy of Canstar Sports Group, Inc., Ontario, Canada.

Today, people expect factory-made products to be safe, attractive and easy to use. They also want products to be well made and designed to meet their needs.

Industrial designers are artists who help companies meet these and other standards for mass-produced objects. An **industrial designer** plans the way a product looks, feels and functions.

Industrial designers must also know about materials and processes for manufacturing. For example, the small, sporty tractor in picture A is an experimental design. This model has many forms molded from strong plastic instead of metal. The plastic parts do not rust and are designed to replace ninety-five metal parts. The fuel tanks are molded into the fenders. What other design ideas can you identify?

The ice skates in picture B are designed as unified sculptural forms. The colors and forms appeal to people who do free-style or dance-like skating. What design qualities would be appealing in ice hockey skates or roller skates?

In the small nation of Denmark, designers have developed a special style of furniture known as **Danish modern**. Picture C shows a Danish modern chair. In this style, the color and grain of wood is carefully selected. The wood is shaped into graceful forms that resemble sculpture. A set of these chairs can be stacked so that they are easy to move or store.

Industrial designers plan products to fit the needs of manufacturers and to please customers. Today, many designers also plan manufactured objects that help to conserve energy and reduce pollution or waste. Can you think of examples of products designed to meet these goals?

Identify a manufactured product that has a design you would like to improve. You may prefer to design a new product that meets your needs or the needs of others. Review some of the criteria, or standards, that a well-designed product should meet. Make sketches or build a model of your industrial design.

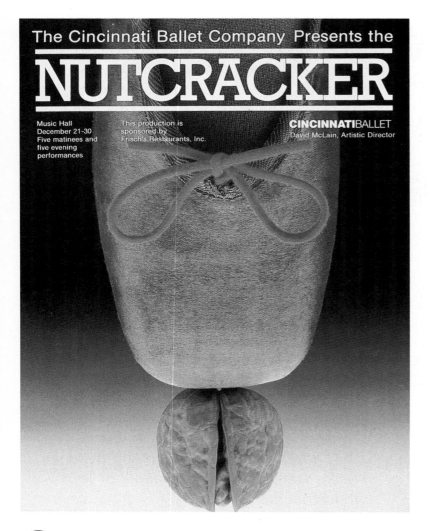

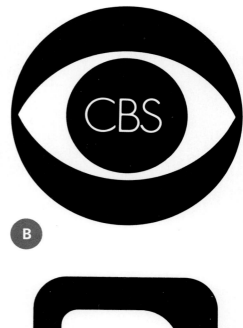

 A   Courtesy of Kauck Photography, Inc., Cincinnati, Ohio.
Photograph: Jeff Kauck.

 C

Graphic designers are artists who plan artwork such as the poster in picture A. They plan the lettering and the images that you see in posters, signs and advertisements. Graphic designers also plan the lettering and some of the artwork for books, newspapers, packages and other things you see.

The graphic designs in pictures B and C are logos. A **logo** is a symbol for a business or a group. People learn to recognize familiar logos. A logo is like a trademark. It can be printed on stationery or used on other objects, such as signs and uniforms.

Postage stamps are planned by graphic designers. The designer creates a **layout** that has all the lettering and artwork for the stamp. The layout for a stamp is usually twelve times as large as the final stamp.

When the layout is finished, it is given to a printing company. Special cameras are

used to reduce the design to the size of a stamp. Then many copies of the design are printed on large printing presses.

Postage stamps can be used to honor important people or events. Sometimes stamp designs honor groups of people, such as nurses or farmers. Some stamps help people remember important ideas, such as protecting endangered animals or working for peace.

Think of a person or an idea that you would like to see honored in a design for a postage stamp. Study some of the sizes and shapes of actual stamps. Sketch several designs. Then create a layout twelve times as large as the stamp.

What should your layout include? What will make your design easy to see? Who or what will your design honor?

Illustration
Styles and Media

 Cover illustration from **The Black Snowman** by Phil Mendez, illustrated by Carole Byard. Illustrations ©1989 by Carole Byard. Reprinted by permission of Scholastic Inc.

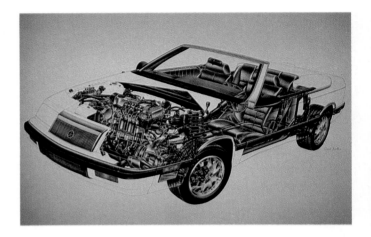

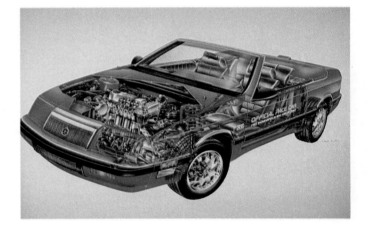

B   **David Kimble,** cutaway views of a car. Courtesy of the artist.

The art of illustration is one of many careers for people who like to draw, paint and take photographs. **Illustrations** are pictures that help to tell a story or explain something. Today, many illustrations are used to help advertise products.

There are many styles and types of illustration. An illustration for a story or poem should capture a mood or feeling related to the writing. Sometimes important characters and events are shown. For the book in picture A, the illustrator made sketches of people and city streets. She tried out several designs.

Picture B shows a **technical drawing** with many details and shading. This illustration shows how the parts fit together. This kind of view is called a **cutaway** illustration. What can this kind of illustration show that a photograph cannot? What are other examples of technical illustration?

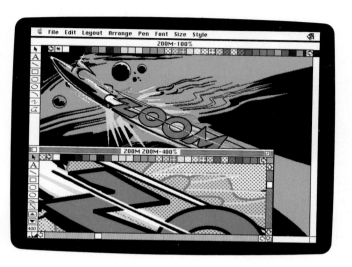

C   **Benedetto Garacci , *Ben Franklin: Birth of Printing.***
©1993 Benedetto Garacci.

D   Courtesy of Apple Computer, Inc.

Today, many illustrations are created by **photographers**. Picture C is a "special effects" photograph. It combines two photographs to create a fantasy image. What story does the photograph illustrate?

The computer is another tool for illustrators. Picture D shows the screen, or monitor, of a computer with a drawing on it. Can you find part of the drawing that is enlarged? Think about artists who use computers. Should they know more about art or more about computers? How could you find out?

Collect and cut out illustrations from old picture magazines. Look for different styles and types. Work with several other students and sort the examples into categories. Discuss your examples and categories with the class.

After you have done your research, create an original illustration in a medium of your choice.

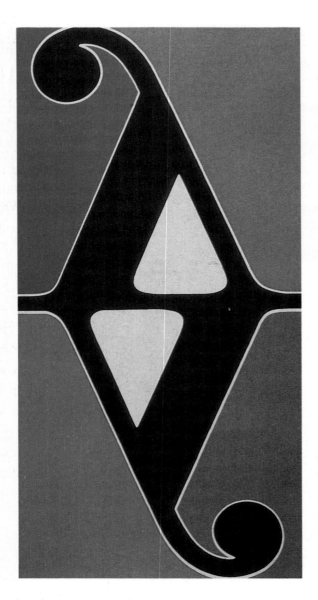

A ***Why the Y,*** designed by Bob Farber. Originally appeared in *Upper & Lower Case, The International Journal of Type and Graphic Design*, March 1983, vol. 10, no. 1, page 42. ©1983, International Typeface Corporation. Used with permission.

B ***A Kaleidoscopic A,*** designed by Bob Farber. Originally appeared in *Upper & Lower Case, The International Journal of Type and Graphic Design,* March, 1983, volume 10, number 1, page 44. ©1983, International Typeface Corporation. Used with permission.

Have you ever made patterns or designs with letters of the alphabet? This is one way graphic designers get ideas for their work. Sometimes their ideas are used for bookcovers, posters or other printed materials.

In picture A you see the letter "y" two times. Each letter is the same but they are combined to create a design with **asymmetrical** balance. If the designer had used this same plan with the letter "H" or "W," would the balance be **symmetrical** or asymmetrical?

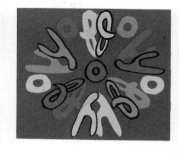

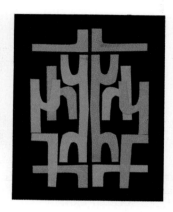

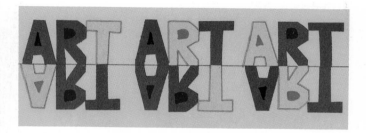

 C **Paul Rand,** Cover illustration for *DADA*, 1951.

D Student artwork.

The letters in picture B are alike in outline, but divided into other colorful shapes. The divisions and colors are different in each letter. The whole design has **radial** balance. The shapes and lines go out from a center.

Let's look at some other ways to use letters. In picture C, you see the title for a book, *Dada,* spelled out in two directions. The dark letters stand out from the light letters and background. The letters are overlapped to create an up and down rhythm and a left to right movement.

Students created the designs in picture D. They chose a **color scheme** for the overall design. Then they practiced lettering. To cut identical letters, they folded lightweight colored paper. Symmetrical letters were cut by drawing one half of the letter near the fold. Be creative. Try your own ways to create patterns and designs with letters.

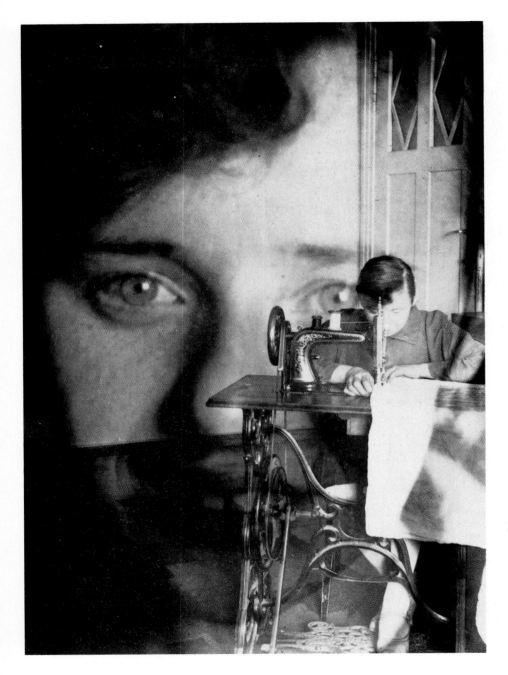

Alice Lex-Nerlinger, *Seamstress,*
ca. 1930. Silver gelatin print, 6 1/2 x
4 5/8" (17 x 12 cm). Julien Levy
Collection, Gift of Jean Levy and the
estate of Julien Levy, 1988.
Photograph ©1991, The Art
Institute of Chicago, All Rights
Reserved.

A woman toils at a sewing machine. She
appears to be alone in a room, but you also
see the large face of a child. What mood or
feeling is communicated to you?

When you look at this artwork, does
the picture make you think about a dream
where parts are real but don't seem logical?
This artwork is a photomontage. A
photomontage is a collage that includes

Romare Bearden, *Carolina Shout,* 1974. Collage with acrylic and lacquer on board, 37 1/2 x 51" (95 x 130 cm). Mint Museum of Art, Charlotte, North Carolina (Museum Purchase: National Endowment for the Arts Matching Fund and the Charlotte Debutante Club Fund).

parts of photographs. When these "pieces of reality" are combined, they create a dream-like quality.

In a photomontage, you can show several ideas or feelings in one picture. You can also suggest how special views of people, places and events can be combined in your memory.

Ideas for a photomontage can be developed in several ways. African-American artist, Romare Bearden, collected and saved photographs that had a special look or meaning. He cut out parts of different photographs and rearranged them several times. Sometimes he added lines and shapes with ink or other drawing media.

Look through old newspapers and picture magazines for photographs. When you find several that are related to a special memory or theme, move them around in different ways and develop a composition. Use one photograph for the **center of interest**, then group and overlap other photographs around it.

 Eadweard Muybridge, *Studies of Horse and Rider,* 1870. Photograph. Courtesy of Sotheby's Inc., 1987.

In the 1860s, Eadweard Muybridge began to make some of the first photographs of the motion of people and other things. The six photographs in picture A show a horse and rider in a fast sequence of motions. His experiments led to the art of **motion pictures**.

In 1895, Thomas Edison invented a **camera** that could record many pictures on a piece of film. When the pictures on the film are shown rapidly, the eyes see a continuous motion.

In the 1920s, Walt Disney and others developed motion pictures called **animations**. In these cartoon-like movies, separate pictures are drawn by artists. The drawings have slight changes in them, such as those you see in picture B. Some animated movies have over a million drawings recorded on a strip of film.

In the 1940s and 1950s, Elliot Noyes Jr. made animated films with figures and landscapes modeled from clay. The clay models could be changed slightly for each photograph and scene in the film. He also used wet sand as a medium for creating animated landscapes.

C Student artwork.

Canadian Norman McLaren discovered that animations could be made by drawing directly on film, without using a camera. He also created animations with objects, such as chairs, that seem to fly and do other tricks.

Most animated films are planned with flip books. A **flip book** is a small book with drawings on each page. You can make a flip book from index cards. The first card shows the beginning of the action. The last card shows the end of it. The other cards are called **tweens**, or in-betweens. The tweens show the transitions, or changes, between the first and last card. After the drawings are made, you flip through the edges of the cards to see the motion.

Picture C shows some pages from a flip book made by a student. The illusion of movement is caused by changing the size, position and proportion of elements. The horizon line and point of view also change.

Many of the visual effects that you see in animations are also used in television. You might do research to learn more about the history of these art forms and many related careers.

Locate Lost Golf Balls

Professor Butts puts his head in a nutcracker and squeezes out an idea to locate lost golf balls.

Hang golf bag (**A**) on hook (**B**) which pulls cord (**C**) and tilts paddle (**D**), tossing basketball (**E**) into basket (**F**). Weight of ball releases hook (**G**) and allows spring (**H**) to push head-guard (**I**) into stomach of toy clown (**J**) who claps cymbals (**K**) on rubber bulb (**L**), squirting stream of water (**M**) which starts phonograph (**N**) playing "Sonny Boy." Song awakens mother love in Snozzle Bird (**O**). She longs for a son and looks around for an egg to hatch until she finds golf ball (**P**) which she naturally mistakes for the coveted egg.

If the Snozzle Bird wants a daughter, have the phonograph play "Ramona."

 Rube Goldberg, *Locate Lost Golf Balls.* Reprinted with special permission of King Features Syndicate, Inc.

Do you like to look at funny pictures? Many people do. Some of the oldest comic pictures show animals dressed up as people. Can you think of present-day cartoons or comic strips that feature animals as characters? Why do you think the theme of animals as people has been so popular for so long?

During the twentieth century, a new **theme** for cartoon and comic art has become popular. It is the theme of inventions and machines in everyday life. The cartoons in this lesson show just a few ways this theme has been explored.

One of the most creative cartoonists of the twentieth century, Rube Goldberg, portrayed people who invent complicated machines to do a very simple task. In many cartoons, a person is shown using ten or twelve connected inventions to roast a hot dog or get a letter from a mailbox. This theme in Rube Goldberg's cartoons became so popular that many people speak of awkward, complicated things as "Rube Goldberg" inventions.

B

Above: *Cartoon of man imprisoned in a computer.*
©Graham Sale.
Left: *Robot and Umbrella Illustration.*
©Marc Rosenthal.

C

Cartoon by Phil Marden, 1988.
Courtesy of the artist.

Study cartoons and comic strips. Then create a cartoon or comic strip around machines or manufactured products. The objects can be characters or your own version of a Rube Goldberg invention.

Your characters in a cartoon might be refrigerators, cars, boats or radios. They could be toasters, dishes or hairbrushes. You might combine several products or machines to create a character. How will your characters interact with each other?

If you like to work with mechanical problems, you might think of an absurd, complicated way to turn off a light switch without getting out of bed. What other simple activities could you use as a subject for this kind of cartoon?

 A   **Jean Williams Cacicedo,** artist's drawing of the front of **Chaps,** 1983. Courtesy of the artist.

 B   **Jean Williams Cacicedo, Chaps: A Cowboy Dedication,** 1983. From *Art to Wear* by Julie Schafler Dale, Abbeville Press. Photograph: Otto Stupakoff. ©Julie: Artisan's Gallery, New York.

Have you ever thought of clothing as a form of art? All over the world, people create and wear clothing. Clothing protects the body. It can keep a person warm or help them stay cool.

Some people believe that clothing should be plain, simple and useful. This way of dressing makes you pay attention to the person more than their clothes. Some people like to make or choose clothes that go with their activities or personalities.

Some contemporary artists design clothing as a form of expression. They create designs that are unique. **Unique** means that only one example of the design is created.

You can see a unique design in the coat on this page. The artist's sketch in picture A shows her idea for the coat in picture B. The design has ideas from clothes worn by ranchers. The back of the coat has elements from a landscape with cactus plants and a fence. Arrows suggest the directions a rancher might travel while herding animals.

Phil Nuytten, *Newtsuit,* 1984. Courtesy of International Hard Suits, Inc., North Vancouver, Canada.

Today, many artists are **clothing designers**. Some specialize in designing clothes for children or other age groups. Some plan clothing for special activities. For example, picture C is a design for a diving suit. The suit is worn by people who explore in deep water or repair underwater equipment.

The costume in picture A is another example of clothing design. **Costume designers** plan the way people are dressed for events such as a ballet, a play, a motion picture or a television show.

Clothing designers often make sketches of their ideas. The sketches may show the front and back view of a design. Sometimes they show the side view too.

Find out more about clothing design in different periods of history and different cultures. Draw several original designs for clothing or costumes. You might research clothing design as a career.

Review Unit 3
Art in Your World

A

1900-1920

1920-1940

Courtesy of Nynex Corporation.

B   **Charles Voysey, *Let us Prey.*** Wallpaper design, ca. 1900.

Joseph Frank, *Primavera Fabric,* ca. 1930.

C   From the Collections of Henry Ford Museum & Greenfield Village.

In this unit, you have learned about many products that artists design. Show what you have learned by describing and analyzing the examples of design you see here.

The symbols in row A are examples of graphic design. What changes do you see in the design of these logos? Why do you think the designs have changed since 1900? Which of the two logos has the most changes from one period to the next?

What are some changes in the fabric designs? Which designs have organic lines and shapes? Which are more geometric in design? Why might some of the older fabric designs still be popular?

1940-1960   1960-present

Courtesy of Aluminum Company of America.

Lucienne Day, "Flotilla" Fabric, 1952.

Fabric design samples by Group of Ten, Sweden, 1972.

What changes can you see in the designs for cars? Why do you think the designs have changed since 1900? What other forms of transportation have been streamlined, or designed with sleek curves, since 1900?

People today have many choices in the designs for a single product. Look through some newspapers or magazines for different designs of automobiles, chairs, lamps and other products. Cut out the pictures and display similar products together. Find out why people like some designs more than other designs.

The artworks in this lesson are **sculptures** created by **assembling**, or putting together, pieces of materials. Some of the materials are ready-made objects, such as wood scraps, empty spools and plastic lids. Materials like these are often called **found objects.**

The sculptures in pictures A and B are made from pieces of wood. Some of the forms are scraps of wood that the artist sands and paints. Some of the parts, such as dowels, come from a store. The pieces are assembled and glued or nailed together.

B **Thomas Kloss, *Father Bird Icon.*** Wood, metal, paint, 76" (194 cm) high. Courtesy of the artist.

A **Thomas Kloss, *Exotic Bird,*** 1988. Wood, metal, paint, 42 x 76" (107 x 193 cm). Courtesy of the artist.

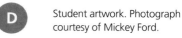
Student artwork. Photograph courtesy of Mickey Ford.

Ann P. Kriner, *Bluebird,* 1991. Painted wood, 8 x 12 x 24" (20 x 30 x 61 cm). Courtesy of the artist.

Inexpensive and easy-to-find materials are used to create artworks in many lands. Low-cost or scrap materials are often used by folk artists. **Folk artists** learn to create art by trying out ideas or watching friends and family create art. The artwork is usually made for their own use or pleasure. The lawn sculpture in picture C was created by a folk artist.

Found materials can be natural things, such as twigs, rocks or shells. They can be old parts from manufactured objects, such as broken toys or empty containers. Many artists enjoy "recycling" discarded materials to create crafts and sculpture.

A student created the sculpture in picture D. What materials were used? How were details added? What kind of personality does the sculpture seem to have?

Collect objects for a sculpture. Any discarded washable object must be cleaned with soap and water before you use it. Hold different objects in several positions to get ideas for the sculpture. If you want to add paint or crayon to parts, do this first. Let the parts dry before you assemble them. Why should you follow these steps?

In this unit, you will learn more about sculpture. You will also learn about crafts of the past and present. A **craft** is a product made with great skill by hand, such as weaving and pottery.

46 Shaping Metal
A Foil Relief Sculpture

A

Warrior and Attendants Plaque, 16th century. Bronze, 15 x 16″ (38 x 41 cm). The Nelson-Atkins Museum of Art, Kansas City, Missouri (Nelson Fund).

B

Oxus, Plaque of Standing Man, 550–300 B.C. Gold. Reproduced by courtesy of the Trustees of the British Museum, London.

The sculpture in picture A was created about 350 years ago in Nigeria, Africa. It was made for the palace of the Oba, or king, of Benin. It is a relief sculpture. **Relief** means that parts stand up from a background. Coins are very small relief sculptures.

The king is shown in the center. He is wearing a tall, beaded collar and many bracelets. On each side are soldiers and children making music. The patterns on their clothing represent designs that were printed on cloth. What other details do you see in this sculpture?

The relief sculpture in picture B is made from a thin sheet of metal. The design was created by **embossing**, or shaping, the metal. The shapes that stand up were pressed into the back of the metal. The deep lines were made by pressing the front of the metal.

This sculpture was created about 2,500 years ago in Babylonia. This land is now the country of Iraq. How is the bearded man dressed? What other details do you see? What do you think they mean?

 D Student artwork.

C ***Heart from Oaxaca***. Painted tin, 9 7/8" (25 cm) high. Collection of Chloë Sayer. Photograph: David Lavender.

Some artists create relief sculptures as gifts or decorations. The decoration in picture C was made in Mexico. The artist cut out the metal shape, embossed it, and added paint. Some artists sell this kind of work to tourists. Art galleries and museums also have collections of these colorful relief sculptures.

A student made the relief sculpture in picture D from metal foil. You can try this process. Make some sketches first.

Begin your sculpture as if you are making a collage. You will need a background shape made of cardboard. Cut out shapes

from thick paper or index cards. Glue the larger shapes down first. Then glue smaller shapes on top of the larger ones. Several layers of paper shapes will create a good relief, or raised design. You can also add yarn, string or fabric to your collage.

When the collage is dry, brush the whole surface with thin, white glue. Center a smooth sheet of aluminum foil over the collage. Gently press it down with your finger tips, working from the center of the design outward. Press the foil carefully so the relief, or raised, surfaces show clearly.

A **Louise Vergette, *Mescalito.***
Papier-mâché. Photograph: Peter Marshall.

The sculpture in picture A was created by a **contemporary**, or present day, artist from England. The form of the dog was made by constructing an **armature**, or support, of wood and wire. Then the armature was covered with papier-mâché.

Papier-mâché is the process of building up a form with strips of paper dipped in a watery paste. When the layers of pasted paper dry, the artwork is firm and hard.

 C

Piñata, Mexico, 20th century. Papier-mâché figure in dress of dyed tissue paper, 33 x 20 x 6 1/2" (84 x 51 x 17 cm). Collection of Mingei International. Photograph: Jim Coit.

You can create a papier-mâché sculpture. For the armature, you need some long pipe cleaners or floral wire. Cover a sheet of newsprint paper with the soupy paste used for papier-mâché. Fold the soggy paper several times. Place a wire on the paper lengthwise. Keep the wire inside and roll the paper tightly into a rod. Make three rods and join them with strips of paste-soaked paper (see picture D). Build up the form with more strips of paste-soaked paper. When the form is dry, you can paint it and add other materials to complete the design.

People in many lands create sculpture in papier-mâché. A Mexican artist created the sculpture in picture B. It is a gift holder called a **piñata**. Candy and small gifts are put inside the piñata. On birthdays, a piñata is hung up, and children take turns striking it with a stick. When the piñata breaks, everyone scrambles for the treats.

D

113

48

Modeling Clay
Sculptured Portraits

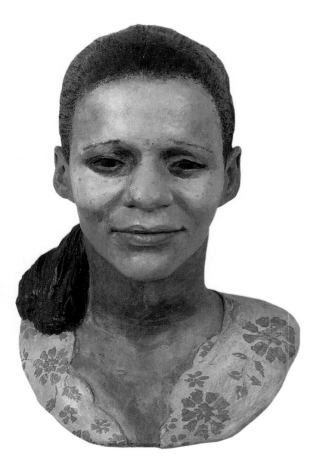

 A

John Ahearn, *Pregnant Girl,* 1979. Oil on cast plaster, 14 x 10 x 7 1/4 " (36 x 25 x 18 cm). Courtesy of Brooke Alexander, New York.

B Malvina Hoffman, *John Keats,* 1958. Marble, life-size. Courtesy of National Sculpture Society.

Portraits of people have been created for thousands of years. In sculpture, a portrait of a person's face often includes the neck and part of the shoulders and chest. These artworks are called **portrait busts**.

Portrait busts can be created in different media. What media have these artists used? Which sculpture was carved? What processes were used to make the other sculptures? How can you learn more about media and processes for creating sculpture?

Notice the **views** of each sculpture. If you could see the real sculptures, you could see them from many views. They are three-dimensional forms. They have height, width and depth or thickness. Which sculpture has been photographed in a front view? Can you find the one **profile**, or side view, of a sculpture? Find the works photographed in a **three-quarter** view. This view is between a profile and a front view.

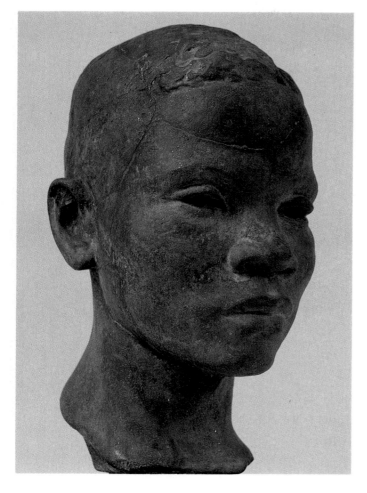

 C

Create a portrait in clay. You might use the steps in pictures E, F and G to begin. To create a self-portrait, look in a mirror or study several photographs of yourself taken from different views.

D

Student artwork.

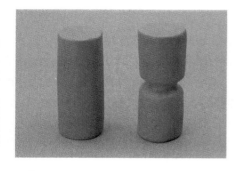

 E

Begin with a cylinder. Pinch it in the center.

 F

Carve and model the forms. Study all the views.

G

Carve details. Use small tools to add texture.

49

Modeling Wire
Sculptures of People

Mahonri M. Young, *Groggy,* 1926 (side view). Bronze, 14 1/8 x 9 3/8 x 8 1/8" (36 x 24 x 21 cm). Collection of Whitney Museum of American Art, New York (Gift of Gertrude Vanderbilt Whitney). Photograph: Sheldon C. Collins, New Jersey.

B **Mahonri M. Young,** *Groggy,* 1926 (front view). Bronze, 14 1/8 x 9 3/8 x 8 1/8" (36 x 24 x 21 cm). Collection of Whitney Museum of American Art, New York (Gift of Gertrude Vanderbilt Whitney). Photograph: Sheldon C. Collins, New Jersey.

You have learned that artists look for lines that show the action and movement of people. Action lines often bend just as parts of your body can bend. If you made a sculpture of an action figure, it should look different in each view. What parts of your body bend or stretch when you run, dance or play?

Study the two views of Mahonri Young's sculpture of a boxer. The diagrams under pictures A and B show how a wire **armature** can be made for similar action figures. Staple the wire to a base. Then build up the form by adding other materials to the wire. For example, you might wrap strips of cloth dipped in glue around the armature. You could build up forms with papier-mâché. Can you think of other ways to build forms around the wire armature?

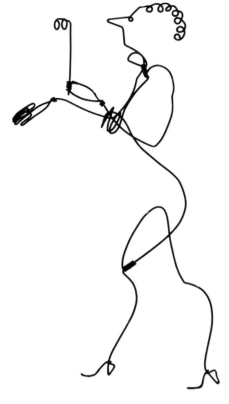

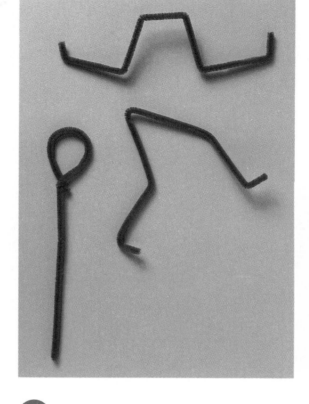

 Alexander Calder, *The Hostess,* 1928. Wire construction, 11 1/2" (29 cm) high. Collection, The Museum of Modern Art, New York (Gift of Edward M. M. Warburg).

D

Alexander Calder created the wire sculpture in picture C. This photograph shows one view of the sculpture. If you looked at the real sculpture, you could see other views, such as the front view and top view. Each view would look different.

You can see open spaces between the wire lines and around the figure. Artists call these open spaces, **voids**, or negative spaces. Artists plan negative spaces very carefully. Can you explain why?

Create a sculpture using wire. Picture D shows how to use three pipe cleaners for a basic "skeleton" figure. Bend your wire into different action poses. Study the lines and negative spaces from all sides.

Decide whether the sculpture will be made just from wire or whether you will add other materials to suggest the forms and clothing.

50

Subtracting Clay
Carving an Abstract Sculpture

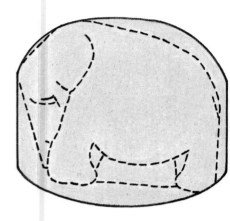

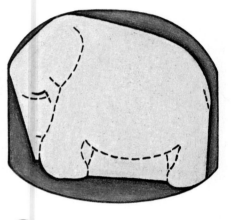

 John Bernard Flannagan, *Elephant,* 20th century. Carved plaster, 7 7/8 x 4 3/4"
(20 x 12 cm). ©The Detroit Institute of Arts (Gift of Robert H. Tannahill).

B

The sculptures in pictures A and C are abstract in style. **Abstract** means that the forms are simple and have few details. Only the most important forms are shown. Even though the forms are simple, you can tell that one sculpture shows an elephant and one shows a person.

The sculptures in this lesson are also carved from solid blocks of material like stone or wood. Carving is a subtractive process. **Subtractive** means that you cut or take away the surface to create the form. In most carving materials, you cannot replace or glue back the materials you have carved away. If you carve very thin parts, the material can break. This is why parts, such as the legs, are thick or pulled in toward the body.

The diagrams in pictures B and D show how sculptors try to "see" a sculpture inside a solid block of material. When John Flannagan carved the profile of the elephant, he had to "see" the form of the block and the parts to be cut away. He had to see, or visualize, each side of the block in this way.

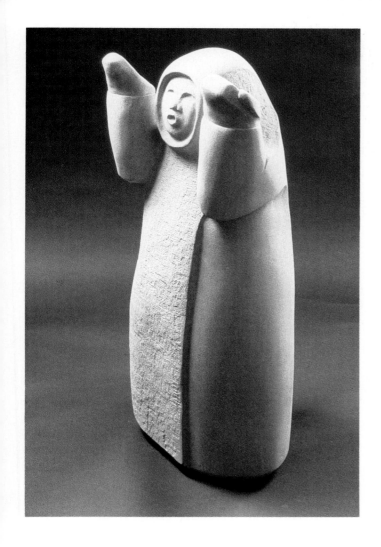

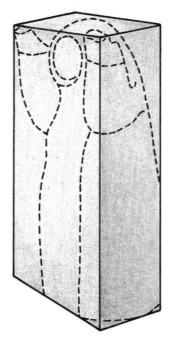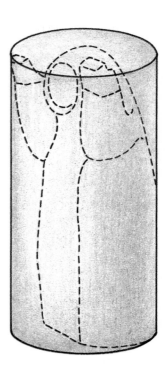

 D

 C Susie Bevins-Ericsen, *Even the Rocks Cry Out,* 1983. Sandstone, 38 x 14 x 12" (97 x 36 x 30 cm). Courtesy of the artist. Photograph: Dennis Hellawell.

Susie Bevins-Ericsen's sculpture in picture C is inspired by her North American Indian heritage. She is an Inuit artist from Alaska. In this work, the artist has carved a figure dressed in bulky clothing with mitten-like hands. She says that many of her ideas come from traditional Inuit activities and legends.

You can practice carving. Create a small abstract sculpture in clay. You might plan your sculpture by sketching a person or an animal from the top, front, back and sides.

Remember that all forms must be thick, simple and close together.

Model your clay into a solid form similar to the overall form of your subject. For example, a standing figure might be carved from a cylinder or tall block.

Use tools such as small sticks, paper clips and butter knives to carve. While you carve your block, imagine that the figure is inside of the block. To uncover the figure, gently cut away the surface on every side of the block. Keep turning the clay so that you can see each side of the sculpture.

 A Isamu Noguchi with *Brilliance*. Courtesy of the Isamu Noguchi Foundation, Inc. Photograph: Shigeo Anzai.

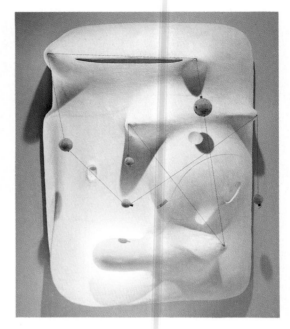

B Isamu Noguchi, *Lunar Landscape,* 1944. Magnesite cement, cork fishing line and electric lights, 33 1/4 x 24 x 7" (84 x 61 x 18 cm). Hirshhorn Museum and Sculpture Garden, Smithsonian Institution, Washington, DC. Photograph: Lee Stalsworth.

Contemporary sculptors work in many styles and with a variety of materials. The artworks in this lesson were created by Asian-American artists. After you learn about these artists, do some research on contemporary artists. Find out how their family heritage, or experiences, influenced their art.

Isamu Noguchi in picture A is known as an inventive sculptor and architect of parks with sculptural elements. The sculptures in pictures B and C show his imaginative and sensitive use of different materials.

Isamu Noguchi was born in Los Angeles, California. His parents took him to Japan for his early education. After high school, he studied sculpture in the United States and Europe. He returned to Japan and China to study ceramics and brush drawing.

Isamu Noguchi has designed large garden-like environments and plazas. One of the largest is in Detroit, Michigan. The fountain is programmed by a computer to create a range of effects, from a fine mist to a thundering column of water.

C Isamu Noguchi, *Big Boy,* 1952. Karatsu ware, 10 1/2 x 6 7/8 x 4 1/2" (27 x 17 x 11 cm) including base. Collection, The Museum of Modern Art, New York (A. Conger Goodyear Fund).

D **Patti Warashina, *Customized Car Kiln.*** Ceramic with wood and leather base, 30" (76 cm) long. Courtesy of the artist.

F **Nam June Paik** with *Tricolor Video*, 1982. Courtesy Gamma Liaison, New York. Photograph: Jean Claude Francolon.

E **Ruth Asawa, *Number 9,*** 1955. Brass wire, 66" (167 cm) high. Collection of Whitney Museum of American Art, New York (Gift of Howard Lipman).

Asian-American artists trace their **heritage** to Japan, China, Korea and many other Asian countries.

Patti Warashina created the ceramic sculpture in picture D. Her work has been shown in many countries. It often combines realism and fantasy in a style known as Surrealism.

Ruth Asawa, who lives in San Francisco, created the woven wire sculpture in picture E. She also works on large ceramic clay projects with her relatives, other artists and children.

Nam June Paik was born in Korea. He lives in New York City. For thirty years, he has created environments with television sets as sculptural elements.

North American Indian Masks
Maskmaking

In almost every country today, you can find a tradition of masquerading, or wearing masks and costumes for special occasions.

The North American Indian masks in this lesson are now in museums. Some North American Indians still make and wear masks to remember their traditions.

The masks in A and B were created by Navajo Indians. Much of this region is a desert.

The two masks were made for special ceremonies in which the Navajo people prayed for a rain spirit to come. The masks have symbols for lightning and corn. Can you explain why?

A

Navajo Ceremonial Mask.
Courtesy of the Department of Library Services, American Museum of Natural History, New York. Photograph: C. Chesek.

B

Navajo Ceremonial Mask.
Courtesy of the Department of Library Services, American Museum of Natural History, New York. Photograph: C. Chesek.

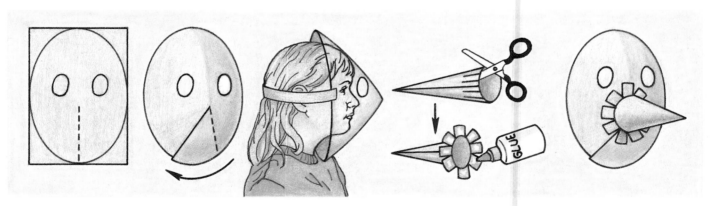

C   You might begin a mask this way. How else can you make it have forms?

The masks in D and E were carved from wood by Kwakiutl Indians who live in the great forests of Canada near the Pacific Ocean.

The masks of the Kwakiutl are made for ceremonies that call for animal spirits to help them be strong and brave.

The Kwakiutl masks are made with movable parts. The jaws are moved by strings inside the mask. Can you find movable parts on the masks in D and E?

D *Mask of the Kwakiutl Indians* of Vancouver Island, British Columbia. Wood with movable parts. Courtesy of the Department of Library Services, American Museum of Natural History, New York.

E *Mask of the Kwakiutl Indians* of Vancouver Island, British Columbia. Wood with movable parts. Courtesy of the Department of Library Services, American Museum of Natural History, New York. Photograph: C. Chesek.

Beautiful Writing
The Art of Calligraphy

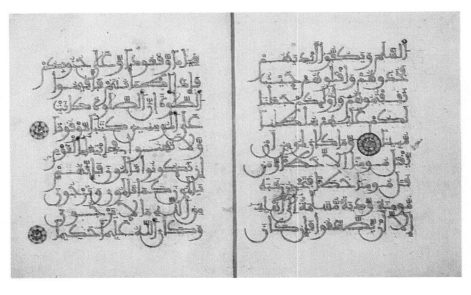

 Text from the Koran, 11th century. Gilt on vellum, 11 x 19" (28 x 23 cm). Reproduced by courtesy of the Trustees of the Chester Beatty Library, Dublin.

 Simon Bening, *Prayerbook of Cardinal Albrecht of Brandenburg,* 1525–30. Vellum, 6 5/8 x 4 1/2" (17 x 12 cm). Collection of The J. Paul Getty Museum, Malibu, California.

Calligraphy is the art of beautiful handwriting. The writing is also carefully placed on the page. The art of calligraphy began with scribes who hand-lettered books for religious teaching. A **scribe** is a person whose handwriting is done with great skill.

The calligraphy in picture A is from the Koran, the sacred book of Islam. The gold seal on the left marks the end of a chapter. Artists who letter such books strive for excellence. They follow a saying of the religious leader, Muhammad: "Good writing makes the truth stand out."

The lettering in picture B is from a Christian prayer book. Books like these were created during the Middle Ages and the Renaissance in Europe. This kind of artwork is called an **illuminated manuscript**.

Traditional calligraphy is done with ink and a quill pen made from the stiff part of a feather. Today, calligraphy pens with points of steel or felt are sold in most art stores. Libraries have books that help you learn various styles of calligraphy.

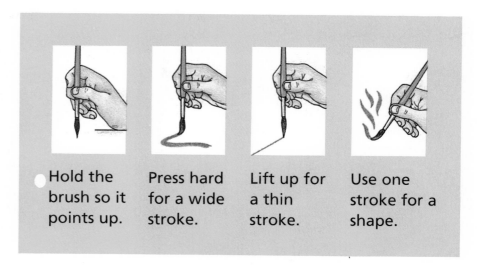

Hold the brush so it points up.

Press hard for a wide stroke.

Lift up for a thin stroke.

Use one stroke for a shape.

D

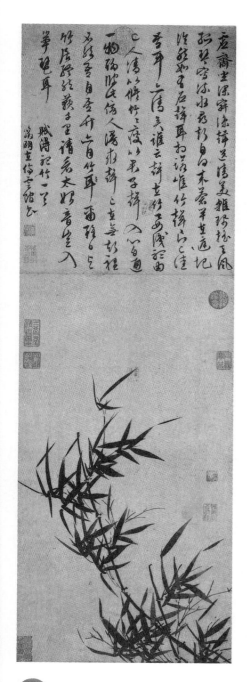

C **Wen Cheng-Ming,** *Listening to the Bamboo,* Ming Dynasty. Hanging Scroll, ink on Sung sutra paper, 38 x 12" (97 x 30 cm). The Cleveland Museum of Art, Ohio (Leonard C. Hanna, Jr. Fund).

In China, Japan and other parts of Asia, calligraphy and painting often go together. The painting is usually created first. Then a poem is added. Part of the poem in picture C says:

The sound of bamboo (is) now very beautiful;
my ears are also clear.
Who says the sound is in the bamboo?
To know it (the sound) depends on oneself.

Practice writing a short poem or quotation. Books on calligraphy show styles and techniques for beautiful writing with a pen or brush. Do some experiments too. Remember these points:

1. Sit or stand with your weight evenly balanced. Take several deep breaths to build up your concentration.

2. Practice making the strokes in the air, then make them on the paper.

3. For brushwork, practice the steps in picture D.

 A Seven examples of recent pottery by the Nampeyo family. Andrews Pueblo Pottery and Art Gallery, Albuquerque, New Mexico.

B Nampeyo outside of her house with Sikyatki Revival Pottery, 1901. Courtesy of the Southwest Museum, Los Angeles. Photograph: Adam Clark Vroman.

 C **Nampeyo,** *Jar,* late 1890s: 13" diameter, 4" at rim (33 x 11 cm); *Bowl,* late 1890s: 9 3/4 x 3" (25 x 8 cm). Courtesy of the Southwest Museum, Los Angeles. Photograph: Craig Klyver.

For thousands of years North American Indians who live in the southwest have created **pottery** for their own use. Around 1880, some families also began to create pottery for sale to tourists and art collectors.

One of the first well-known Hopi potters, Nampeyo, is shown with some of her work in picture B. Look at the bowl in her hand and the large jar in the upper right corner. The same artworks are in picture C.

Nampeyo taught her children and grandchildren the art of making pottery. This **tradition** continues. In picture A, you see recent work by Nampeyo's descendants.

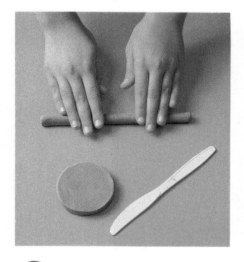  

The designs in North American Indian art show a deep respect for nature. Hopi designs often have symbols for rain, lightning, clouds and flowing water. Other visual symbols show important crops such as corn, blossoms of squash, and beans on vines. Birds, snakes and other animals are also included.

North American Indians of the southwestern United States often use the **coil method** to create pottery. A coil is a rope-like piece of clay at least 1/2" (1 cm) in diameter. The coil method is a step-by-step process.

1. Make a base for the pot. Press clay into a flat slab about 1/2" (1 cm) thick. Trace a circle on the slab. With a table knife, cut out the circle and save the extra clay.

2. Prepare slip to join pieces of clay together. **Slip** is a creamy mixture of water, clay and a few drops of vinegar.

3. **Score**, or scratch, some fine lines on the top edge of the base. Brush slip on top of the scored area. Make a coil. Bend and

press it down on the slip. Cut the coil so the ends meet.

4. Add more coils. Score and add slip to each coil before you join them together. Blend the coils together on the inside. If you wish, you can smooth the outside too.

5. While the clay is moist, you can press textures or patterns into it. What tools could you use? You can add small dots or coils of clay for a relief design.

6. Allow the clay to dry. If your clay is to be **fired**, your teacher will arrange for this.

Practice making coils and joining them before you begin. Try out ways to make textures and patterns too. These experiments will help you think and get ideas for pottery.

Will you create a vase, a bowl or a jar? What other forms might you consider? Think about the "personality" of your pot. Could it be graceful? humorous? mysterious? What proportions and other design ideas should you consider?

 Sarah Hass, *Log Church Snow Scene,* 1979. Quilt, 34 x 41" (86 x 104 cm). ©1979 Sarah Hass. Courtesy of the artist.

People have made quilts for thousands of years. A **quilt** is like a blanket with several layers of cloth. Pieces of cloth are stitched together to create a design. Tiny stitches hold the pieces of cloth together. Do you know people who make quilts? What makes a hand-made quilt different from a blanket purchased at a store?

There are many styles of quilts. The quilt in picture A is done in a pictorial style. The design is like a large picture. This quilt shows a village church in the snow. The border design is carefully spaced to look like a frame. The stitching is planned to create textures and to outline important shapes. What else has the artist carefully planned? What other details make this a well-crafted quilt?

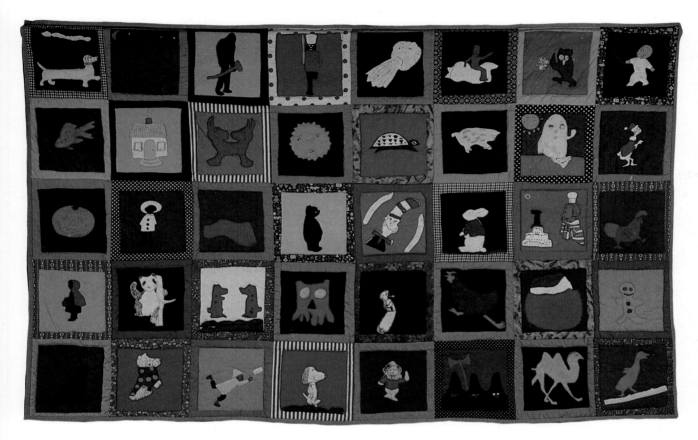

Students in a fifth-grade class created the quilt in picture B for their school. It illustrates favorite characters and symbols from books these students read. Everyone in the class created one square for the quilt. Quiltmaking is now a tradition in this school. Every year, a new quilt is made and displayed in the school or community.

Notice the plan for the whole quilt. The main character in each square is large, simple and on a plain background. These choices help to unify the work. They also help you to see each character or symbol.

How have the students created variety in their own squares and in the whole quilt?

Think about a theme for a quilt. A theme is a main idea that can have many examples to illustrate it. Identify ways to unify the whole quilt.

You can make a quilt-like mural from collage designs. For a final or permanent quilt, use cloth, yarn or thread. You can sew buttons, ribbons and the like to the cloth. Plan and create one square for a class quilt. Everyone should make squares of the same size.

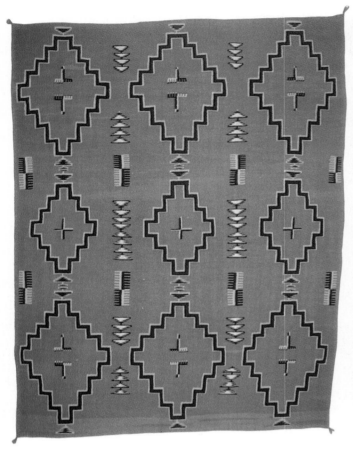

A

Navajo Late Classic Serape, ca. 1870. Raveled flannel and bayeta field, indigo blue, anilin yellow, 52 1/2 x 68 3/4" (133 x 175 cm). Hozhó Gallery, Crested Butte, Colorado.

B

Lori Kammeraad, ***Newsprint,*** 20th century. Dyed wool, 44 x 55" (112 x 140 cm). Courtesy of the artist.

Most of the cloth, or fabric, you see in stores is woven on looms. A **loom** is a frame that holds many pieces of thread, called the **warp**, very straight. A loom is used so that other threads, called the **weft**, can be woven over and under the warp threads.

Thousands of years ago, people in Africa, China and the Americas created simple looms to weave cloth by hand. This tradition of weaving cloth by hand continues in many lands.

Today handmade weavings are often displayed as works of art. The serape, or cape, in picture A was first created by a Navajo artisan as clothing. An **artisan** is a person who has mastered traditional ways to design and make a work.

The weaving in picture B was created by a fiber artist. A **fiber artist** knows traditional techniques for using yarn-like materials, but combines techniques in his or her own way. This artist created a textured,

Bouake weaver setting up his loom before securing it on the tree support. Photograph: Jacqui Holmes.

Kente cloth. Photograph: Jacqueline Robinson.

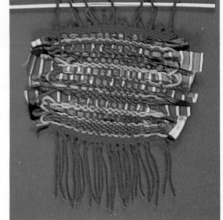
Student artwork.

flowing, abstract design. This kind of work is a **wall hanging**.

On the Ivory Coast of Africa, men are responsible for weaving Kente, a ceremonial cloth used for scarfs and robes. The cloth is woven in long strips. In picture C a man is preparing a loom to weave a Kente design like you see in picture D. Boys learn to weave **Kente cloth** at the age of eight or nine.

You can create a cardboard loom for weaving. Mark the top and bottom of cardboard every 1/4" (6 mm). Make a short cut or notch at each mark.

Wind string up and down so it fits in each notch. You have put the warp on your loom.

Cut yarn, ribbon or strips of cloth for the weft. Weave these over and under. Push the weft close together.

When you have finished, turn the loom over. Cut the middle of the strings. Carefully tie these together at the top edge of your work. Then tie all the bottom strings. The ends can be the fringe or border.

A   ***Neirika.*** Acrylic yarn on wax-covered board, 23 5/8" (60 cm).
Collection of Chloë Sayer. Photograph: David Lavender.

B   ***Neirika*** (detail).

In many cultures, artists are changing their traditional art forms in order to earn money from their special art skills. This kind of art is often sold in stores that specialize in importing arts and crafts. Examples of this kind of art are seen in pictures A-C, created by the Huichol Indians of Mexico.

For hundreds of years, the Huichol Indians have created paintings made of yarn. These yarn paintings, called **neirikas**, are placed at shrines where people pray.

The word neirika refers to the face or countenance of a spiritual force. The themes in Huichol yarn paintings include many gods and natural events. Common symbols include the moon, sun, deer, snakes and flowers.

In the last twenty years or so, the Huichol Indians have discovered that other people admire their neirikas. Today many neirikas are made for art galleries and tourists instead of shrines. The artworks still show Huichol symbols but the designs are made to please the people who buy them.

Votive gourd: Flood, as described in Huichol mythology. Gourd lined with glass beads pressed into wax, 8 1/4" (21 cm). Collection of Chloë Sayer. Photograph: David Lavender.

D Student artwork.

Traditional neirikas are made on a board covered with wax. Yarn is pressed into the soft wax to outline the design. More yarn is pressed down to fill all of the space.

The Huichol also create bowls and trays for religious offerings. The bowl is covered with wax. Glass beads are pressed into the wax in designs that tell religious stories.

Today, many neirikas and bowls created for export are made with glue instead of wax. The artworks also have thicker yarn or beads than the traditional crafts. In addition, other artists from Mexico are creating yarn paintings for tourists.

You can appreciate the skill and patience needed to create a yarn painting by trying this process. A student created the artwork in picture D by gluing yarn to cardboard.

Be sure to plan a simple design and fill all of the spaces. Use glue in a squeeze bottle. Squeeze a thin line of glue around the main shapes in your design. Press the yarn into the glue gently. Keep your fingers free of glue by wiping them on a damp paper towel. It is best to practice first.

Mosaics are pictures or designs made from small pieces of colored glass, stones or other materials. The pieces are glued down side by side. In glass or stone mosaics, the spaces between the pieces are filled in with plaster.

In this lesson, you will create a mosaic from paper that you prepare as shown below.

1. Make six stripes of different colors. Make each stripe about the same width.

2. Use the same six colors to add six stripes across the first ones. Your paper should look like this, with thirty-six colors. Cut your paper so that each color is a separate piece for your mosaic.

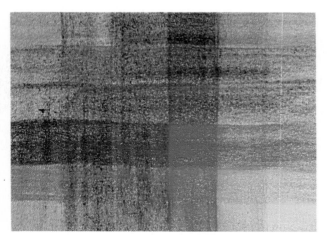

Mosaic artworks are made up of small patches of colored materials. The patches of color are side-by-side, but they seem to blend when you see them from a distance. Can you explain why this happens?

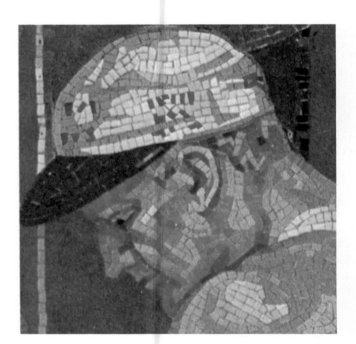

 A

 B

Look at the pattern of light and dark colors in pictures A and B. How does the artist create the illusion of highlights and shadows in the mosaic?

Pictures A, B and C are details from mosaic murals created by Winold Reiss for a railroad station in Cincinnati, Ohio. The murals were completed in 1933. When part of the railroad station was closed, the murals were restored and placed in the airport.

The mosaic in picture D is more than 1,700 years old. It was found in Antioch, a city in Turkey. Antioch was once the capital of ancient Syria. Similar mosaics were created in other lands near the Mediterranean Sea.

Create a small paper mosaic from the pieces of paper you have colored. You can cut or tear them into smaller pieces. Paste the pieces down side by side, like puzzle pieces. You might use one of your sketchbook drawings for your design.

C **Winold Reiss,** mosaic created for a railroad station, 1933. Photograph courtesy of Greater Cincinnati Airport.

D ***House of the Boat of Psyches, Daphne, Bust of Thetis on a Marine Background,*** 3rd century A.D. Mosaic of naturally colored stone of tessarae, 6'4" x 4'6" (19.3 x 13.7 m). The Baltimore Museum of Art (Antioch Subscription Fund).

135

Crafts Then and Now
Stained Glass

Some traditions of making art are passed along to artists over many years. You can see from pictures A and B that artists of today may use materials and techniques discovered long ago.

The detail of the **stained glass** window in picture A was created about 500 years ago for a church in Reims, France. The window is now in a museum. Windows like this illustrated stories from the Bible. Some

of the windows showed knights and other people who helped to build the church and pay for it.

Contemporary, or present-day, artists continue to make stained glass artwork for places of worship, libraries, stores and homes.

The many small panels in picture B were designed by students for their school. A professional artist who works in stained glass used their designs to create the permanent display.

B Stained glass, 450 student-designed panels, St. Anne's Episcopal School, Denver, Colorado. Leaded and orchestrated by artist-in-residence, Judy Gorsuch Collins. ©Judy Gorsuch Collins.

A *Crucifixion,* detail of a window from St. Remi, Reims, ca. 1190. Stained glass, approximately 12' (366 cm) high.

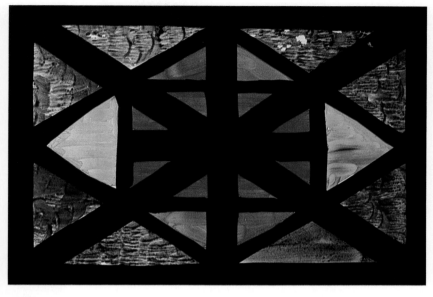

Student artwork.

 Student artwork.

Most pieces of stained glass are transparent or translucent. A **transparent** color allows you to see through it clearly. A **translucent** color lets you see light coming through, but you cannot see details on the opposite side.

The black lines in stained glass are strips of metal that hold the glass. The metal strips are **opaque**. You cannot see through them. These lines are always planned as part of the design.

You can create a design that has translucent color and strong black lines similar to stained glass.

Cut black paper and a plastic folder the same size. First, make sketches on paper the same size as your folder. In your sketches, show the wide black lines that connect with each other and the border. Make the border and black lines about as wide as your index finger.

Redraw your best design on the black paper. Cut out the shapes between the lines. Carefully put paste on the back of the black paper and slip it into the folder.

Put the folder on newspaper so that you see the pasted side of the black paper. Paint over the plastic so the colors will show correctly when the design is seen from the front.

 Photograph: John Senzer for the Fashion Institute of Technology.

People in many lands have created **jewelry**. The tradition of creating rings, bracelets and necklaces goes back for thousands of years. Today, many artists create jewelry as a form of art and to express ideas. The college student in picture A is learning to shape metal to create a bracelet.

In many ancient cultures, artists created jewelry from gold, silver and rare stones, called gemstones. The jewelry in picture B was discovered in the ancient city of Ur in the region of present-day Iraq. The finely-crafted artworks were created over 4,000 years ago.

Notice the patterns created by spacing the beads and shaping thin wire. What other design qualities do you see? Have you seen contemporary jewelry with similar qualities of design?

In cultures where people live very close to nature, jewelry is often made from rare or very colorful natural objects. Feathers, shells, rocks and seeds may be used as media.

 Unknown, *Lady Pu Abi's Cloak Beads on Display.* Near East, Ur, 2650–2550 B.C. The University Museum, University of Pennsylvania.

 C ***Kuba Headband,*** Zaire, ca. 1890–1910. Raffia, cotton cloth, cowrie shells, glass beads, 17″ (43 cm). Courtesy of the Peachblown Collection.

The headband in picture C was created by an artist in Africa. Headbands like these were a symbol of royalty in the Kuba culture. Elaborate shell and beadwork is still created by artists in Zaire and other regions of Africa.

Bead-like jewelry can be created in a variety of media. The media and techniques illustrated in picture D are often used by folk artists. A **folk artist** is a person who has little training in art but is very creative.

You might create a beaded necklace, headband, belt or bracelet. What other types of jewelry could you create? What design elements and principles should you remember as you plan your work?

Some Ways to Create Beads

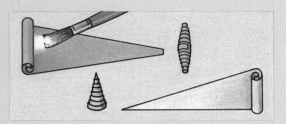

1. Cut strips of colorful pictures from magazines. Apply glue. Roll up the paper tightly. Let the beads dry.

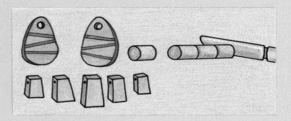

2. Make coils or flat strips of clay. Cut pieces of the same size or vary the sizes to create a rhythm.

3. Dip string into glue. Shape the string on top of wax paper on cardboard. Let the pieces dry.

D

Photograph: Rebecca Wible.

Photograph: Rebecca Wible.

The students in pictures A and B have permission to create drawings on their school playground during the summer. They are working together. The special chalk they are using will wash away with the rain. How can you find out about summer art activities in your community?

There are many places to see artworks in your community. Most shopping malls and many neighborhoods have art shows. Recreation centers often sponsor art shows too. You can see murals, sculpture and other large artworks in parks or lobbies of buildings.

C

D

The students in picture C are visiting an art museum. Most art museums have a **permanent collection** of artworks. Many museums also sponsor special exhibitions of artworks. A special exhibition is usually on display for a short time.

Museums show **original** artworks of different types and styles. Some museums have artworks from many cultures and time periods. Others specialize by collecting work from a particular culture, nation or time. What kind of original art would you like to see?

Your class can plan and put together an art show. It should include artwork by every student. You might invite your friends and family to see the show.

Planning an art show is a group project. With your teacher and classmates, discuss the space for the show and ways to judge artworks. Plan the whole project so that everyone can help make the show a success.

Art Safety

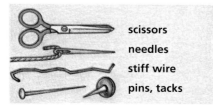

scissors
needles
stiff wire
pins, tacks

Understand and follow all safety instructions your teacher gives you. The following points are important.

• Some art materials can irritate open sores, cuts or a rash on your skin. Do not use clay, oil pastels and other materials that may hurt or infect a skin irritation.

• Some people are allergic to dusty art materials. If you have an allergy, tell your teacher. You might wear a dust mask or use a non-dusty material.

• If you have paint, paste or other art materials on your hands, use a damp paper towel to remove it. Before you eat food, be sure to wash your hands with soap and water.

• The art materials that you use at home and at school should be nontoxic. A label on the material will say nontoxic. Read any label that says "Caution." Understand and follow the steps for safe use of the material.

• Some materials for artwork are empty or discarded containers like boxes, plastic cans and bottle tops. Make sure that all used containers are cleaned before you use them.

• If your work space is neatly organized, you can prevent accidents. Pick up crayons and other materials on the floor. If you spill a liquid, quietly clean it up.

• Hold and use sharp or pointed materials so you do not injure yourself or others. Safety glasses must be worn if you are using wire or any material that may harm your eyes.

Ways to Help in Art

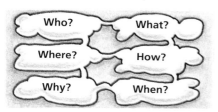

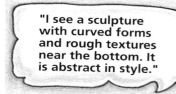

Study these examples of ways to help in art lessons. With your teacher and classmates, develop a list of other ways to be helpful.

• Wear an apron or old, large shirt to protect your clothes. Button the shirt in the back and roll up the sleeves.

• Help to clean up by stacking and putting art materials away neatly. Wash brushes and store them with the hairs pointing up. Collect and save usable materials such as broken crayons.

• Save your artwork in a portfolio. Keep a sketchbook or an art notebook. Write your name and the date on your artwork. This will help you evaluate what you have learned.

• When you discuss art, ask thoughtful questions. Listen and think about the ideas. In art, there is often more than one good answer to questions.

• Learn to combine art words so you can share ideas. Use a dictionary or the glossary to find the meaning of terms. Use the index to find lessons with art terms. What other resources can you use to learn about art?

• Mount your best work.
1. Place your artwork on the background paper.
2. Make sure the borders are even. Trace around the corners.
3. Paste the work down.
4. Make a label on an index card.

Name: _____
Title of work: _____
Materials: _____
I learned: _____

Artists and Artworks

Glossary

abstract (AB-strakt). Not realistic. Artists often add or omit elements in an observed scene to create a simple design.

Abstract Expressionism (AB-strakt ek-SPRESH-un-ism). A style of art. The artist abstracts, or leaves out, details and tries to capture the main action or feeling in a subject.

advance (ad-VANCE). To move forward; the illusion that lines, shapes or colors move toward you.

all-over design (awl OH-ver de-ZINE). A pattern that is repeated across a surface, as in fabrics, carpets and wallpaper.

analogous (ah-NAL-uh-gus). A color scheme planned around colors that are next to each other on the color wheel, such as yellow-green, yellow and yellow-orange.

animation (an-ah-MAY-shun). Cartoon-like movies in which separate pictures are drawn by artists and recorded on long pieces of film or tape. When the film is shown very quickly, the drawings appear to be in motion.

architect (AR-ki-tekt). An artist who designs buildings.

architecture (AR-ki-tek-chur). The art and science of planning buildings and environments for people.

armature (AR-muh-chur). A wire or stiff support that is placed inside a sculpture to hold it up.

art career (art kuh-REER). A job in art that requires special skills and education.

art critic (art KRIT-ik). A person who shares his or her thoughtful judgments about art.

artisan (AR-ti-zun). A person skilled in creating hand-made objects.

artist (AR-tist). A person who plans and creates artwork for a purpose.

assemble (ah-SEM-bul). The process of joining objects, or parts of objects, together.

asymmetrical (AY-sim-eh-trick-al). Artwork that looks balanced when the parts are arranged differently on each side.

border (BOR-der). An edge around a shape, usually wide enough to look like a frame.

brayer (BRAY-er). A small roller that is used to apply printer's ink to a block.

brushstroke (BRUSH-strohk). A definite mark or textured area made with a paintbrush.

calligraphy (kah-LIG-ruh-fee). Beautiful handwriting.

camera (KAM-ur-uh). An instrument used to take photographs.

caricature (KAR-ah-kuh-chur). An artwork that exaggerates how something actually looks, usually in a humorous way.

center of interest (SEN-tur of IN-trist). The main, or first, thing you notice in an artwork.

ceramics (sir-AM-iks). The art of making objects of fired clay.

close-up (KLOHS-up). A view that looks very near or close.

clothing designer (KLOH-thing di-ZIH-nuhr). An artist who designs hand-made or manufactured clothing. Often called a fashion designer.

coil method (koyl METH-uhd). Using long, round pieces of clay to create artwork.

collage (koh-LAHZH). Artwork made by pasting pieces of paper or other materials to a flat surface.

color scheme (KOL-er skeem). A plan for using colors. (*See* analogous)

conservator (kon-SER-vah-tor). A person who protects rare and old artworks from decay and damage.

constructed environment (kon-STRUKT-ed en-VIE-ruhn-ment). Everything people have added to nature or done to alter the natural environment.

contemporary (kon-TEM-puh-rare-ee). Art of the present day or art created very recently.

contour (KON-toor). The edge of a shape.

cool colors (kool KOL-ers). Colors that remind people of cool things; blue, green and violet.

costume designer (KOS-toom de-ZINE-er). An artist who plans what people in a ballet or a play will wear during a performance.

craft (kraft). Skill in creating things by hand. Artwork created carefully by hand.

Cubism (KYOOB-ism). A style of art in which shapes or forms seem to be divided into parts and recombined so that the parts are seen from different views.

curator (CURE-a-tor) A person who gathers information about each artwork in an exhibition and helps decide how to display it.

cut-away (CUT-ah-way). An illustration that shows how the parts of an object fit together.

diagonal (die-AG-uh-nal). A line or edge that slants or tilts.

docent (DOH-sent). A guide and teacher for people who visit the museum.

edge (edj). A line that helps you see a shape, ridge or groove.

elements of design (EL-uh-ments of de-ZINE). Parts of an artwork that an artist plans; line, color, texture, value, space and shape.

embossing (em-BAWS-ing). The process of shaping a relief surface, such as metal, by pressing on it from the front and back.

etching (ECH-ing). The process of scratching into a surface.

Expressionism (ek-SPRESH-un-ism). A style of artwork in which the main idea is to show a definite mood or feeling.

Expressionist. (*See* Expressionism)

exterior (ek-STEER-ee-ur). Outside, or the outside of a form.

facade (fah-SAHD). The whole front wall of a main entrance to a building.

fantasy art (FAN-tah-see art). Artwork that is meant to look unreal, strange or dream-like.

fiber artist (FIE-ber AR-tist). An artist who uses thread-like materials to create artwork.

fired (FIE-erd). Made hard by great heat, as a clay object.

flip book. A small book of drawings that show each step in a sequence of movement. You flip the edges of the pages to see the motion.

folding screen (FOLD-ing skreen). Panels that stand upright in an accordion-like position.

folk artist (fohk AR-tist). A person who makes art for their own use or pleasure, usually without training.

found objects (found OB-jekts). Materials that artists find and use for artwork, such as scraps of wood, metal or ready-made objects.

Futurism (FYOO-chur-ism). A style of art that developed in Italy during the early 1900s. Artists decided to explore motion, speed and energy as themes in 20th-century life.

geometric (jee-oh-MEH-trik). A shape or form that has smooth, even edges.

gesture drawing (JES-chur DRAW-ing). A drawing made quickly to record the main paths of movement or action lines.

glaze (glayz). A mixture of water and colored minerals applied to ceramics. When a glazed work is fired, the minerals melt and create a glassy coating.

graphic designer (GRAF-ik de-ZINE-er). An artist who plans the lettering and artwork for books, posters and other printed materials.

guideline (GIDE-line). A line, folded edge or other mark that serves as a guide for planning an artwork.

harmony (HAR-mo-nee). The arrangement of elements in an artwork that creates a feeling of unity.

heritage (HER-i-tij). The history and culture of a group of people.

highlight (HI-lite). A very bright area of light reflected from a surface.

horizon line (hor-I-zuhn line). The line where the sky meets the ground.

horizontal (hor-i-ZON-tal). A straight line that lies flat.

hue (hyoo). The common name for a color, such as red, yellow, blue, orange, green, violet.

illuminated manuscript (ih-LOO-muh-nayt-ed MAN-yu-skript). A book, decorated with small, detailed illustrations, from the Middle Ages in Europe.

illusion (ih-LOO-zhun). In art, a design that causes you to think an image is real.

illustration (il-uh-STRAY-shun). A picture that helps to tell a story or explain something.

illustrator (IL-uh-stray-tor). An artist who creates pictures for books and magazines.

imagination (ih-maj-uh-NAY-shun). The process of creating a mental picture of something that is unlike things one has seen.

Impressionism (im-PRESH-un-ism). A style of art in which the main idea is to show changes in the light, color or immediate activity of scenes.

industrial designer (in-DUS-tree-al de-ZINE-er). An artist who designs cars, dishes, toys and other products that are made in factories.

interior design (in-TEER-ee-ur de-ZINE). The art of designing the rooms and other indoor spaces of a building.

interior designer (in-TEER-ee-ur de-ZINE-er). An artist who plans the inner spaces of a building.

intermediate colors (in-ter-MEE-dee-it KOL-ers). Colors, such as red-orange and yellow-orange, that are mixed from a primary and a secondary color.

jewelry (JOO-el-ree). Objects, such as rings, necklaces, bracelets and earrings, that are worn for personal adornment.

Kente cloth (KIN-tay klawth). Woven strips of cloth used for ceremonial scarfs and robes in the Ivory Coast, Africa.

kiln (kill). A special oven or furnace that can be heated to a high temperature.

landscape architect (LAND-skayp AR-ki-tekt). An artist who plans parks, gardens and other outdoor spaces.

layout (LAY-out). A plan showing the placement of elements for a finished work of art.

lighting. (*See* illuminate)

line. The path created by a moving point, such as a pencil point.

logo (LO-go). A visual symbol for a business, club or group.

loom. A frame used to hold yarns while weaving.

media (*See* art media)

medium (*See* art media)

miniature (MIN-ee-ah-chur). A very small version of a real object.

model (MOD-el). A person who poses for an artist. Also, small artwork that shows how a larger artwork might look.

Modern Danish (MOD-urn DAY-nish). A style of industrial design developed in Denmark.

monoprint (MON-oh-print). A print that is usually limited to one copy.

mosaic (moh-ZAY-ik). Artwork made with small pieces of colored stone, glass or the like.

motion picture (MOH-shun PIK-chur). An art form in which many pictures are recorded on a long piece of film. When the film is shown rapidly, the eyes see a continuous motion.

movement (MOOV-ment). Going from one place to another or a feeling of action in an artwork.

natural environment (NACH-ur-al en-VIE-run-ment). A setting in nature that has not been changed by humans.

natural stone (NACH-ur-al stone). Any stone found in nature; not manufactured such as concrete or brick.

negative shape or space (NEG-eh-tiv shape or space). Shapes or spaces surrounding a line, shape or form.

neirika (nay-ear-EEK-ah). An ancient art form of the Huichol Indians in Central America; a painting made of yarn.

neutral colors (NEW-trel KOL-ers). In artwork, neutral colors are brown, black, white and gray.

Nonobjective (non-ob-JEK-tiv). A style of art in which the main ideas or feelings are expressed with colors, lines and so on. The artwork does not show objects or scenes.

obvious (OB-VEE-uhs). Easy to see.

Op. A style name for artworks that have optical illusions. A short word for optical.

opaque (oh-PAKE). Not allowing light to go through; the opposite of transparent.

organic (or-GAN-ik). Organic forms are similar to forms in nature and usually have curved or irregular edges.

original (oh-RIJ-en-al). Artwork that looks very different from other artwork; not copied.

papier-mâché (PAY-per–ma-SHAY). The process

of building up a form with strips of paper dipped in a watery paste. When the layers of pasted paper dry, the artwork is firm and hard.

parallel (PAR-ah-lel). Lines that are spaced evenly next to each other without touching.

pattern (PAT-urn). Lines, colors or shapes that are repeated over and over in a planned way. Also, a model or guide for making something.

permanent collection (PER-mah-nent koh-LEK-shuhn). Artworks in an art museum that are not loaned to other museums.

perspective (per-SPEK-tiv). Artwork in which the spaces and distances between objects look familiar or "real."

photographer (foh-TOG-ruh-fur). A person who takes photographs using a camera.

photomontage (foh-toh-mon-TAWZH). Parts of different photographs combined in one picture.

piñata (peen-YAH-tah). A Mexican gift holder made of papier-mâché.

Pop art (pop art). Pop is a short word for popular. A style of artwork that includes advertisements or other popular, often-seen images.

portrait (POR-trait). Artwork that shows the likeness of a real person.

portrait bust (POR-trait bust). A sculptured likeness of a person's head, neck and chest.

pose (pohz). A special way to stand or sit.

positive shape or space (POZ-i-tiv shape or space). Shapes or spaces that you see first because they stand out from the background.

pottery (POT-er-ee). A container created by hand from ceramic clay.

primary colors (PRI-mear-ee KOL-ers). Colors from which others can be made: red, yellow and blue. (In light, the primary colors are red, green and blue).

principles of design (PRIN-suh-pals of de-ZINE). Guides for planning relationships among visual elements in artworks; balance, rhythm, proportion, pattern, unity and variety.

print. A copy of an image, usually made by pressing ink onto paper. Also the process of copying an image in this manner.

profile (PRO-file). Something seen or shown from the side view, such as a profile of a head.

proportion (pro-POR-shun). The size, location or amount of something as compared to that of something else.

quilt (kwilt). A hand-made blanket that is made by sewing pieces of cloth together.

radial (RAY-dee-al). Lines or shapes that spread out from a center point.

Realism (REE-ah-liz-em). A style of art that shows objects or scenes as they might look in everyday life.

realistic (ree-ah-LIS-tik). Portraying subjects with life-like colors, textures and proportions.

recede (ree-SEED). To appear to move away from a viewer, such as colors and shapes in an artwork.

relief (ree-LEEF). A three-dimensional form, viewed from only one side, in which surfaces stand up from a background.

relief sculpture (ree-LEEF SKULP-chur). Sculpture that stands up from a flat background.

replica (REP-luh-kuh). A model, or copy, of a

three-dimensional form.

scientific illustration (sih-uhn-TIF-ik il-uh-STRAY-shun). An accurate, highly-detailed picture used for scientific study.

score. To mark, scratch or roughen a surface.

scribe. A person with great skill in handwriting.

sculptor (SKULP-tor). An artist who creates sculpture.

sculpture (SKULP-chur). Three-dimensional artwork made by carving, modeling or joining materials.

secondary colors (sek-on-dair-ee KOL-ers). Colors that can be mixed from two primary colors; orange, green, violet.

self-taught artist (SELF-tawt AR-tist). An artist who has developed a skill without formal training. Often called a folk artist.

shade. A color mixed by adding black. A dark value of a hue, such as dark blue.

shadow (SHAD-oh). A dark area where there is little light.

shingles (SHING-gulz). Thin boards used to cover the roofs or sides of buildings.

sketch (skech). A drawing that is made to record what you see, explore an idea or to plan another artwork.

slip. A creamy mixture of clay, water and a few drops of vinegar used to stick pieces of clay together.

space. An empty place or surface, or a three-dimensional area in which something exists.

spacing (SPACE-ing). The area between lines and shapes.

stained glass (staynd glass). Pieces of colored glass that are fitted together like parts of a puzzle, then framed to make a window.

stencil (STEN-sell). A paper or other flat material with a cut-out design that is used for printing. Ink or paint is pressed through the cut-out design onto the surface to be printed.

still life (still life). An artwork that shows non-living things, such as books, candles and so on.

stipple (STIP-uhl). Small dots on a surface that create a fine texture.

studio (STOO-dee-oh). The place where an artist creates artwork.

style (stile). An artist's special way of creating art.

subject matter (SUB-jekt MAT-er). The topic or idea in an artwork.

subtle (SUH-tle). Very slight changes, as in color, form or other visual elements.

subtractive (sub-TRAK-tiv). Cutting or taking away the surface to create the form, as in carving wood.

Surrealism (sir-REAL-ism). A style of art in which familiar subjects are distorted into dream-like images.

symbol (SIM-bul). Lines, shapes or colors that have a special meaning.

symmetrical (sih-MET-trik-al). A type of balance in which both sides of a center line are exactly or nearly the same. Also known as formal balance.

technical drawing (TEK-ni-kul DRAW-ing). A

very precise drawing used to explain a complex object.

technique (tek-NEEK). A special way to create artwork, often by following a special procedure.

theme. A story or big idea that artists can interpet in many ways with different subjects.

three-dimensional (THREE-di-men-chen-al). Artwork that can be measured three ways: height, width, depth (or thickness). Artwork that is not flat.

three-quarter view (THREE-KWAR-ter view). A view that is between a profile and front view.

tint. A light value of a color; a color mixed with white.

tradition (tra-DISH-en). The handing down of information, beliefs or activities from one generation to another.

transparent (trans-PAR-ent). Possible to see through, such as a clear piece of glass.

tweens (tweenz). Drawings that show the change between one action and the next in a sequence of drawings.

two-dimensional (TOO-di-MEN-chen-al). Artwork that is flat and measured in only two ways: height and width.

unique (yu-NEEK). Unlike any others.

unity (YU-ni-tee). The quality of having all the parts of an artwork look as if they belong together or work together.

value (VAL-yu). The lightness or darkness of a color (Pink is a light value of red).

value scale (VAL-yu scale). A drawing that gradually shows the shades of gray between white and black.

vanishing point (VAN-ish-ing point). A vanishing point is the place where the edges, lines or shapes in a scene appear to go toward one point and then "vanish" from sight.

vertical (VUR-ti-kul). Lines that go straight up and down.

view. The parts of a scene or object that you can see from a certain position.

viewfinder (VIEW-find-er). A sheet of paper with a hole in it, used to "frame" a scene. On a camera, the lens that lets you see what you will photograph.

visual rhythm (VIS-yu-al RITH-um). Repeated shapes, colors and other visual elements that remind you of rhythms in music or dance.

void. (*See* negative spaces)

wall hanging. (*See* tapestry)

warm colors (warm KOL-ers). Colors that remind people of warm things. Varieties of red, yellow and orange.

warp (warp). In weaving, the threads or yarns placed on a loom and stretched tightly so that other threads can be woven across.

weft (weft). Yarn that is woven horizontally over and under the warp on a loom.

woodcut (WOOD-kut). A relief print created by carving into a smooth block of wood, inking the wood, and pressing paper against the ink.

Index